D0432306

SHADES
OF GREY

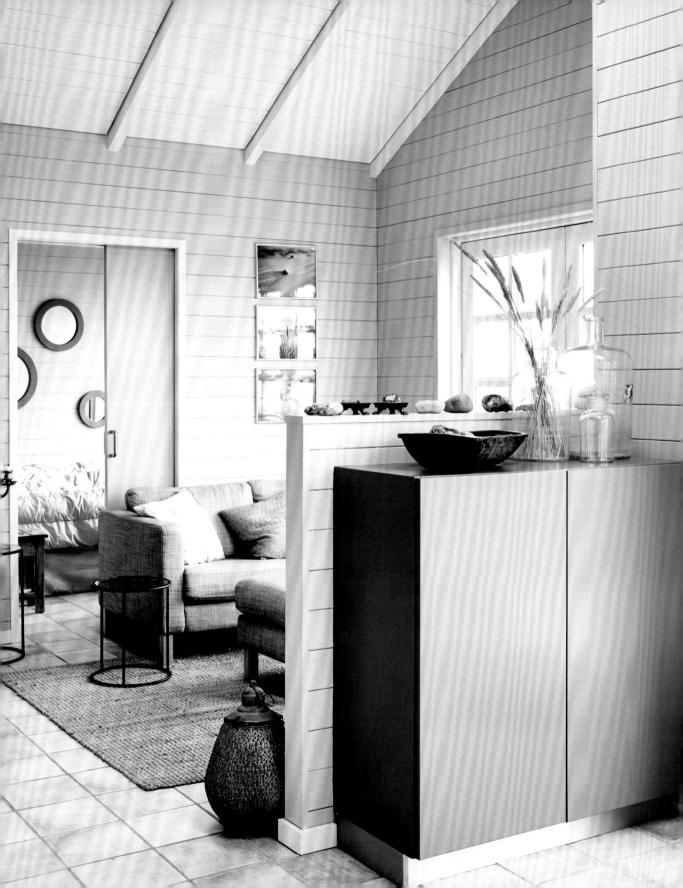

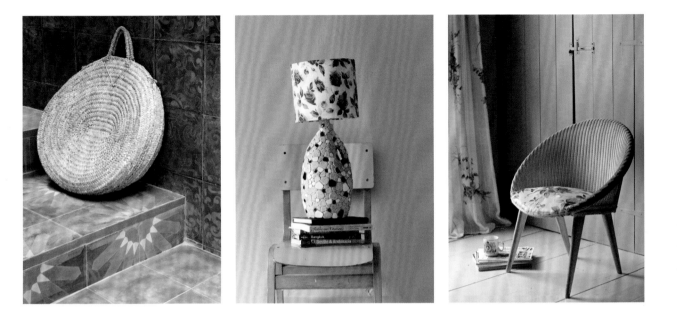

SHADES
OF GREY

DECORATING WITH THE MOST
ELEGANT OF NEUTRALS

KATE WATSON-SMYTH

RYLAND PETERS & SMALL
LONDON • NEW YORK

SENIOR DESIGNER Toni Kay
SENIOR COMMISSIONING EDITOR Annabel Morgan
PICTURE RESEARCH Christina Borsi
PRODUCTION MANAGER Gordana Simakovic
ART DIRECTOR Leslie Harrington
EDITORIAL DIRECTOR Julia Charles
PUBLISHER Cindy Richards

First published in 2016.
This revised edition published in 2019 by Ryland
Peters & Small
20–21 Jockey's Fields, London WC1R 4BW
and
341 East 116th Street, New York, NY 10029
www.rylandpeters.com

10 9 8 7 6 5 4 3 2 1

ISBN 978-1-78879-124-3

A CIP record for this book is available from the
British Library.

Library of Congress CIP data has been applied for.

Printed and bound in China

CONTENTS

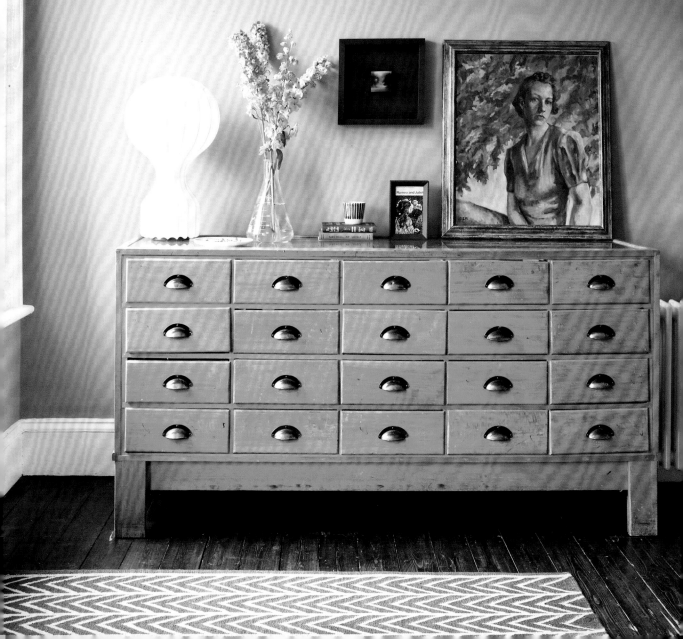

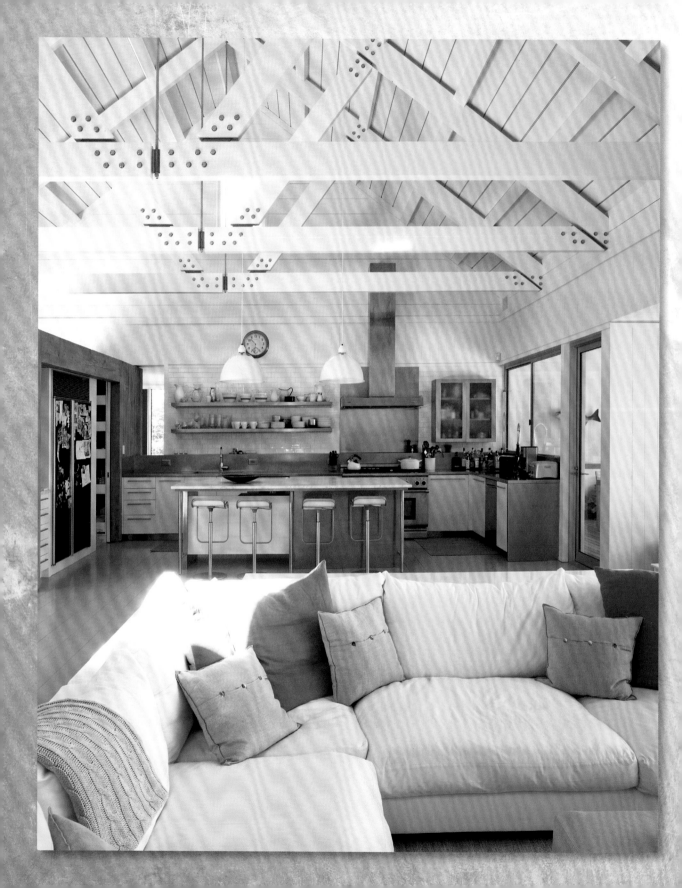

INTRODUCTION

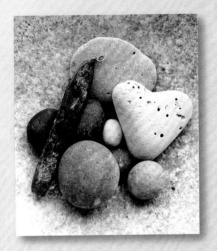

There's no doubt about it, grey is the shade of the moment. Restaurants, shops and homes are coated in it. There's not an interior decorating programme that doesn't use it. And never mind 50 shades – the human eye can, it's been claimed, detect more than 500. As can the average paint chart. And if you thought the whole grey thing was about to be over, I refer you to global paint giant Dulux, who have just expanded their range of greys and now offer 557 in total. "Everyone wants to paint their houses grey at the moment," says Karen Haller, a colour expert who teaches industry professionals the science of applied colour psychology, "but it's one of the most difficult shades to get right because of the colours that lie beneath."

No wonder that in past years we all just slapped a pot of cream paint on the wall, then hastily turned on the TV. But everything's changed now. To start with, we're much more design-savvy. And the global economic crisis has meant that, for the first time in years, we're decorating our homes to live in them and not just to be attractive to prospective buyers. A decade ago, we redecorated every three years; it's now between every five to seven years. So we need to actually put some thought into our choice of paint colour and work out what we like, because we are going to be living with it for a while.

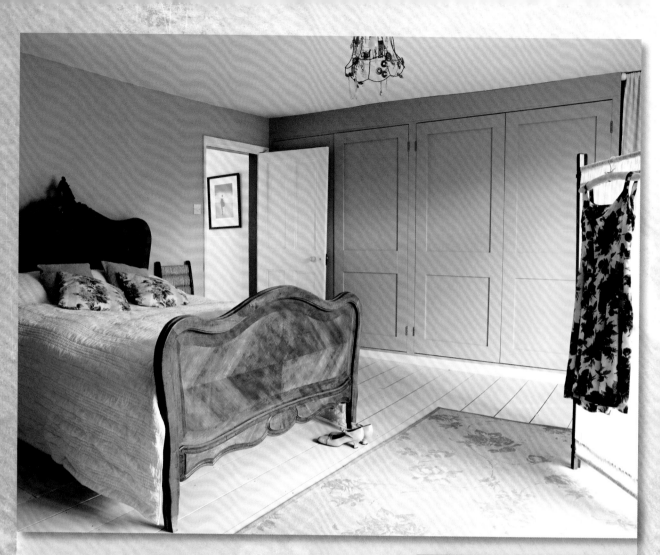

Nowadays, entire careers are built on colour consultancy, psychology and therapy. There are specialists and technologists where once there were simply painters and decorators. Research, albeit of the very unscientific 'let's-just-check-on-Twitter' variety, shows that amateur decorators (that's you and me) try an average of nine different shades before they get it right. And the final colour, which may look grey on the wall, is probably called smoky blue. That's if it's not referencing small furry animals, Hollywood film stars or dead fish.

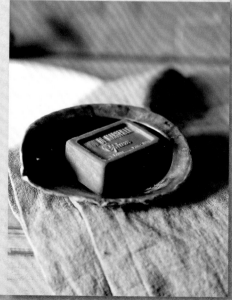

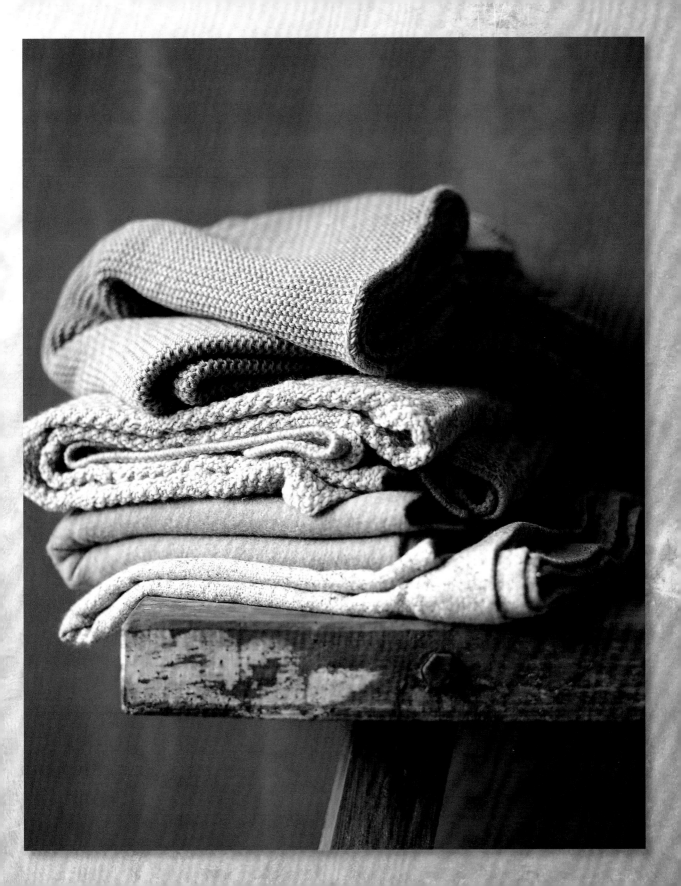

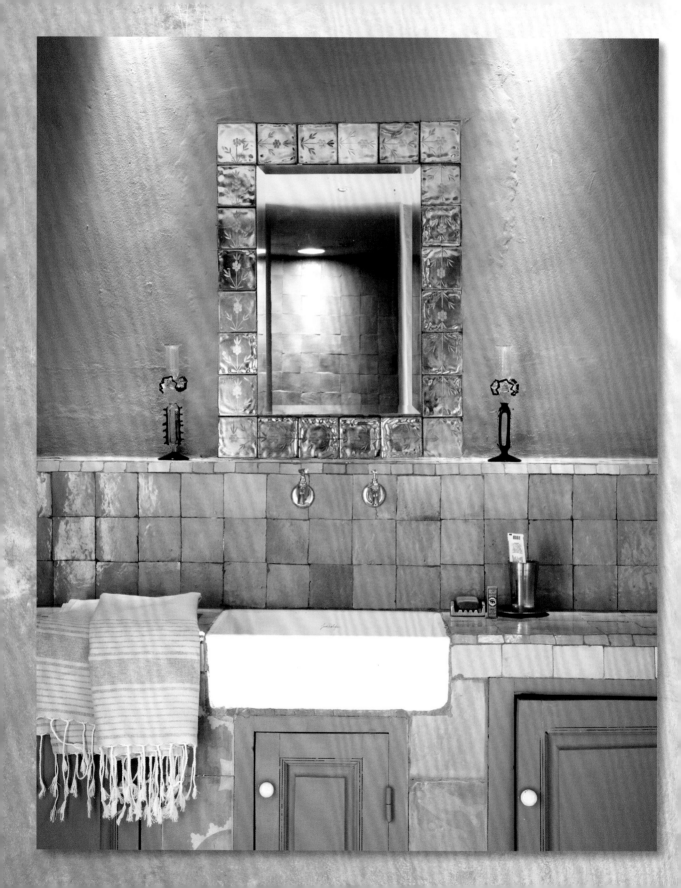

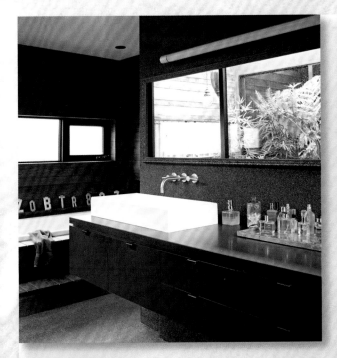

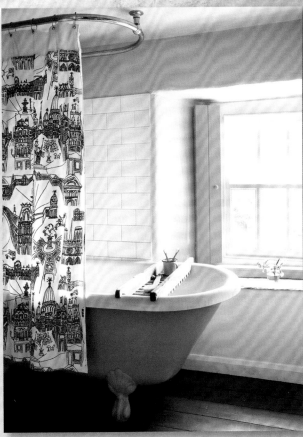

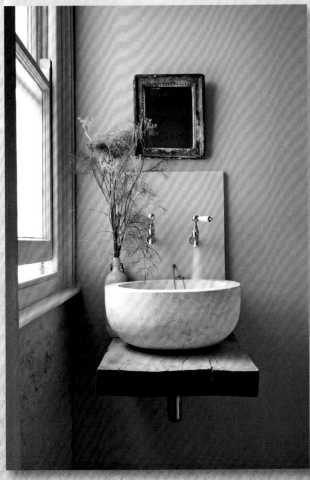

Shades of Grey will reveal the difference between grey and gray and discover why it has become such a dominant trend in modern interiors. No blushes will be spared in sharing other people's (oh all right, my) mistakes so that you can get it right. We will discover, once and for all, how to use those pesky sample pots to best advantage, and whether it's worth splashing the cash on pricey paint. Armed with this book, you'll be able to find the perfect shade of grey, and you can put the money you save on sample pots towards going somewhere hot and sunny, where grey is the colour furthest from your mind…

"Context is everything: you never see grey in isolation. There will always be other colours around it from furniture, paintings, or a person's possessions, so it will always change in different environments.**"**

Simon March, *founder of Colour Makes People Happy*

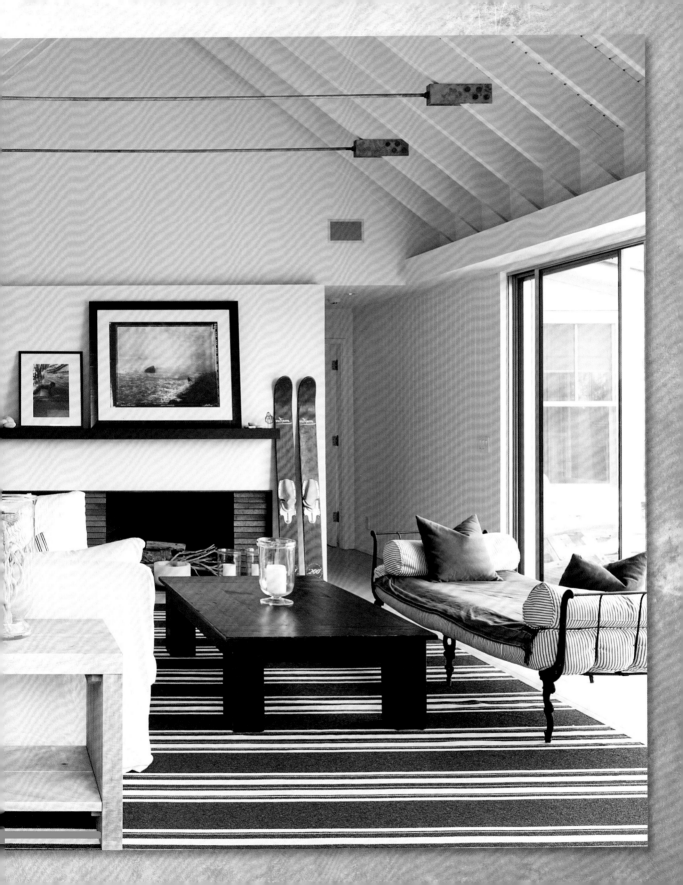

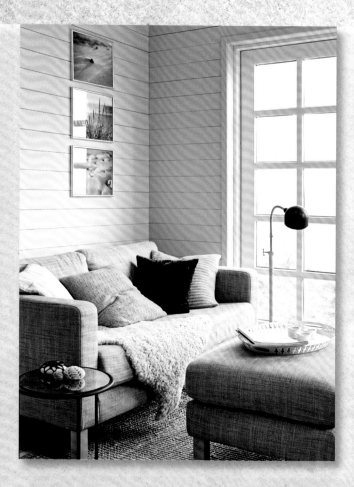

GOING GREY

Grey is no passing fad. But it is one of the hardest colours to get right when it comes to decorating your home. To find the best shade, you need to consider which direction your room faces, what time of day you will be in there, the prevailing weather (even the hemisphere makes a difference) and last of all (in fact, let's be honest, least of all) the actual shade you like.

At this point, I should issue an apology to all those who were expecting something a little racier on the subject of shades of grey.

No, this isn't that book. But you may well get a little breathless when you realize that you can't paint your north-facing sitting room in Gauze (as the entire family will sink into a depression) but have to make do with Mole's Breath instead.

So how do you choose the right shade of grey? It's not as simple as buying a pot of paint and slapping it on the wall. If it were that easy, you wouldn't be reading this book. If it were that easy, I wouldn't have had to write this book just so that I can finish decorating the kitchen.

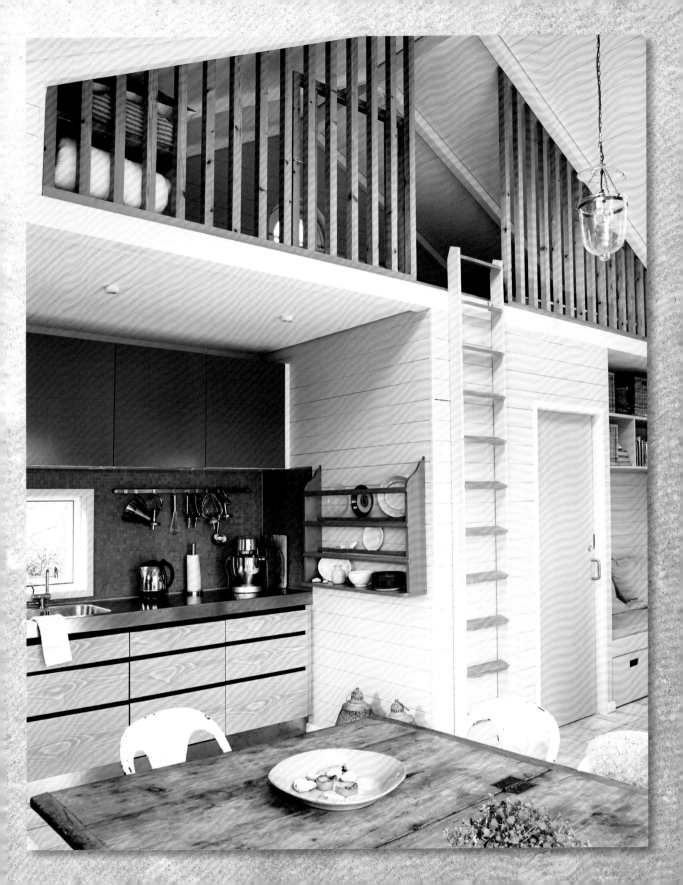

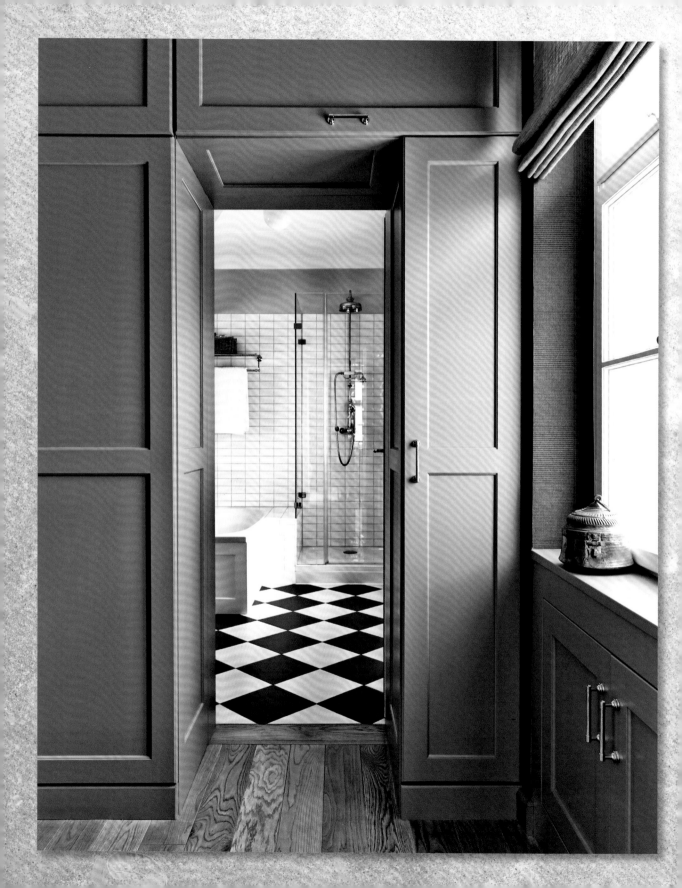

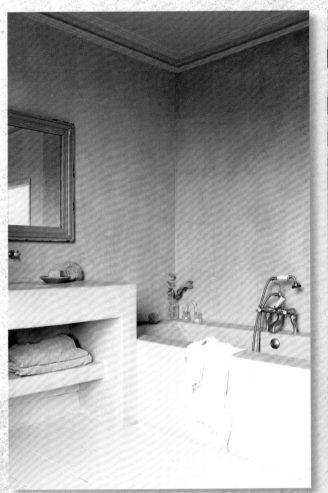
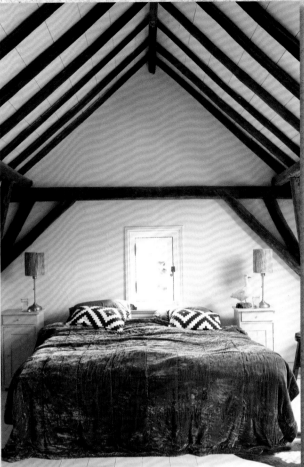

Grey Tadelakt bathroom designed by photographer Paul Massey.

When you drift into the paint shop with a view to grabbing a colour chart, you are confronted with hundreds, even thousands, of options. Most of them look roughly the same to the untrained eye, but they all have different (usually meaningless) names. "Grey?" you say casually to the sales assistant, hoping for a steer towards the dark, mid- or light variety. Instead of which, you find yourself plunged into a tangle of adjectives, obscure historical references and basic biology (who knows what colour an elephant breathes anyway?). Will that be Silver Fox, Mole's Breath

or Bunny? What about Blackened (which is actually pale blue), Clooney (as in George) or (raises eyebrow sardonically) Urbane? You might prefer Timeless... or Urban Obsession?

It doesn't stop there. Do you want that in a heritage range? Gloss, matt or eggshell? Are you going to paint all four walls or just one? Which colour will you pair with it? And will it go with your sofa? (Because, let's face it, after all the money you've spent on paint you're unlikely to be buying a new one of those any time soon.)

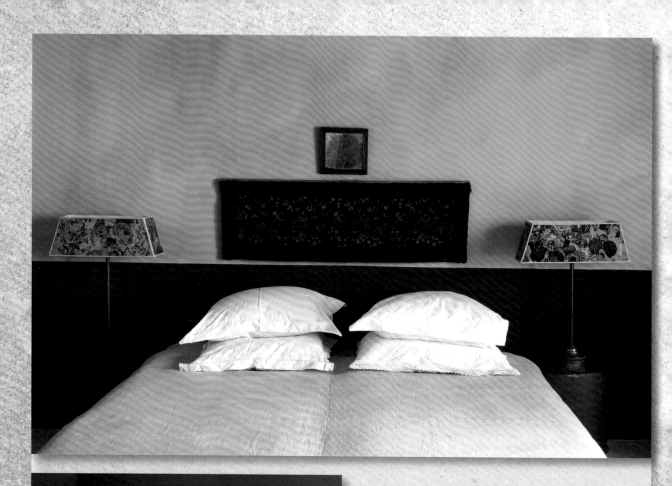

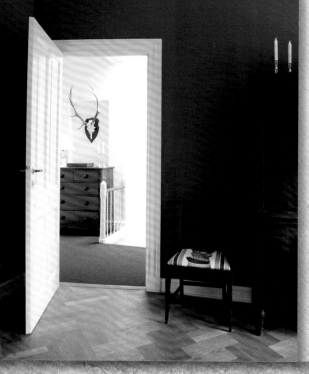

So at last you've chosen a grey. There's been a row. Some sulking. Possibly even a few tears. But, finally, it's done. Now all you need to do is to cover the walls in it. Cut to three days later. The grey that looked so beautiful in the tin has turned your hallway into a prison corridor. It's made your kitchen so cold that you can't afford the heating bills. And who said it was grey? It looks distinctly lilac, now you come to mention it. Back to the shop you trudge for another sample pot…

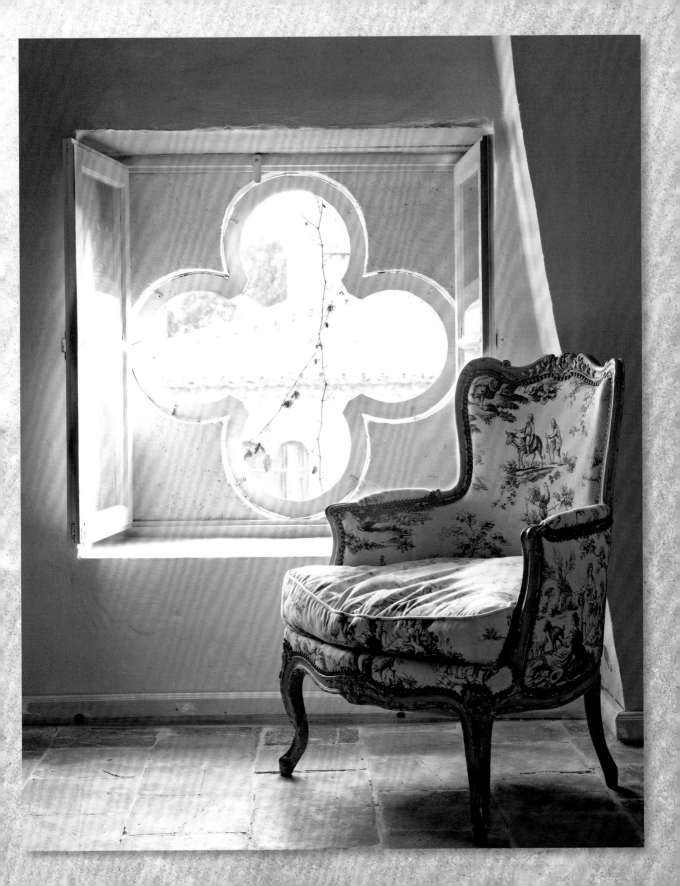

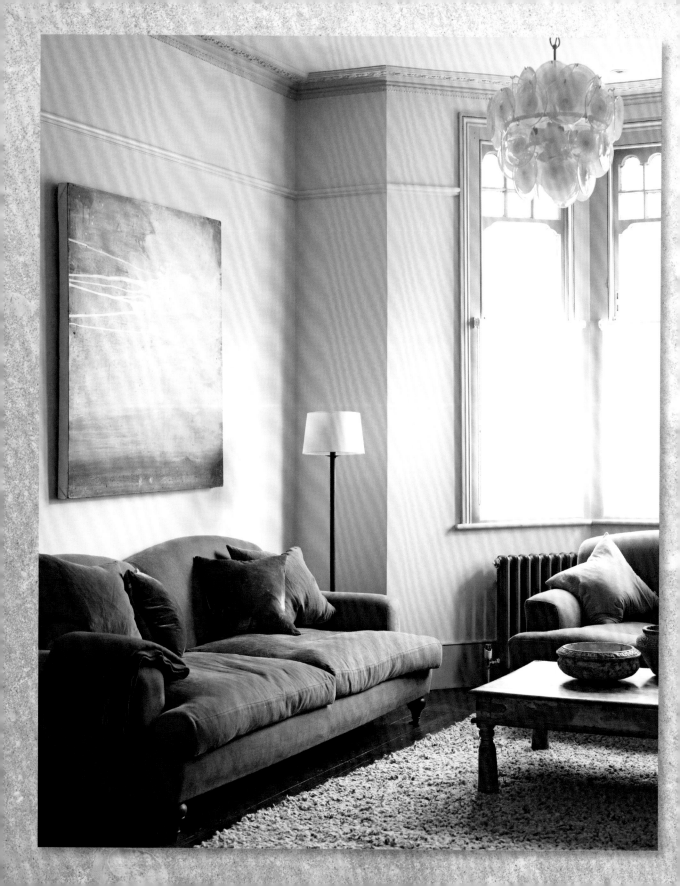

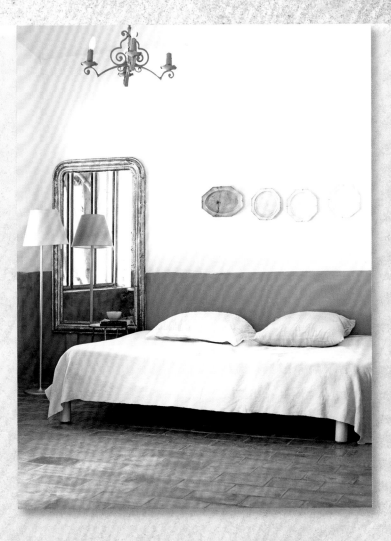

So, as we have seen, making the decision to go grey is the easy part. Once you have decided on that, the possibilities start to multiply like a swarm of locusts.

As Amy Wax, former president of the International Association of Color Consultants and creator of the Color911 app, which allows you to find a paint colour from a photo, says: "Choosing grey has to take into consideration warm light, cool light and the amount of sunlight. What makes the grey palette so challenging is that there are so many factors to keep in mind."

One interior designer admitted to me (completely off the record) that she used to try at least five different shades per wall and the only reason she gets it right now is that she sticks to one shade of grey from one paint brand. That way, she reckons, she has learned exactly how it will react in any given space.

Perhaps it's no surprise to hear that other professionals use exactly the same trick. They gather about ten different shades, usually from different companies, and they 'learn' them. Which is fine and dandy for

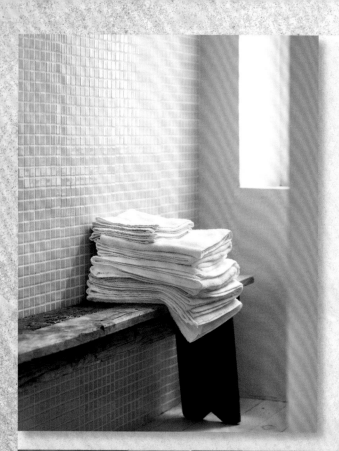

them, but doesn't really help the rest of us. As the US stylist and TV presenter Emily Henderson says, "I've probably painted over 50 rooms in the last couple of years, so I've learned a thing or two." As opposed to the rest of us, who have simply painted the same room 50 times in 50 different shades.

So for those of us who just want to finish painting the sitting room, move the sofa back into place and go back to thinking about what to have for dinner, what can we do to avoid any painting pitfalls and minimize the mistakes? This book aims to guide you towards choosing exactly the right shade of grey. Just read on, and you will (hopefully) find out.

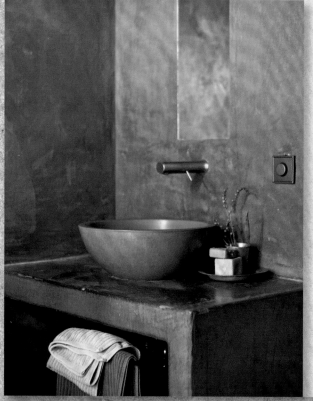

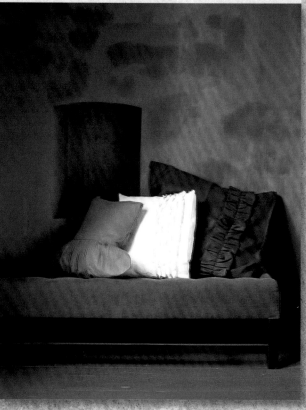

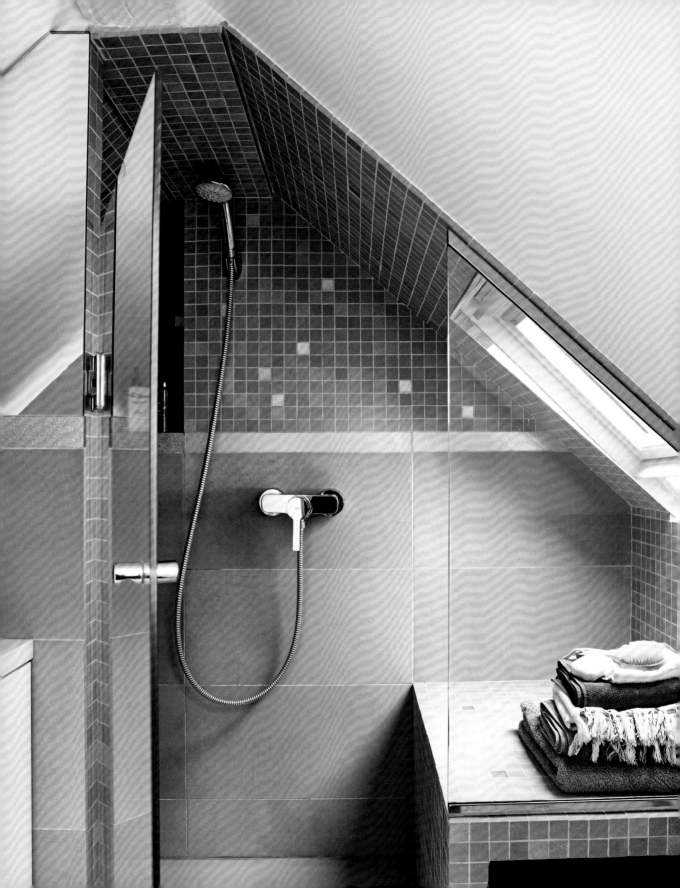

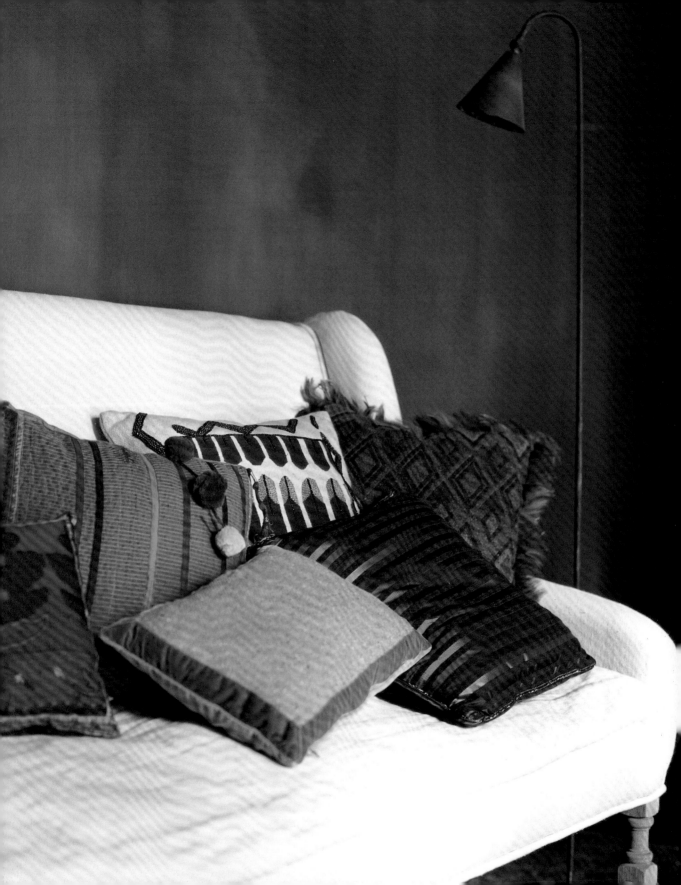

Ivory Black, a 19th-century black paint, was made by burning the ivory from offcuts of the comb-making industry. Sold in blocks, it mixed well with white lead to create a beautiful pearly grey colour. So, environmentally disastrous and possibly poisonous as well.

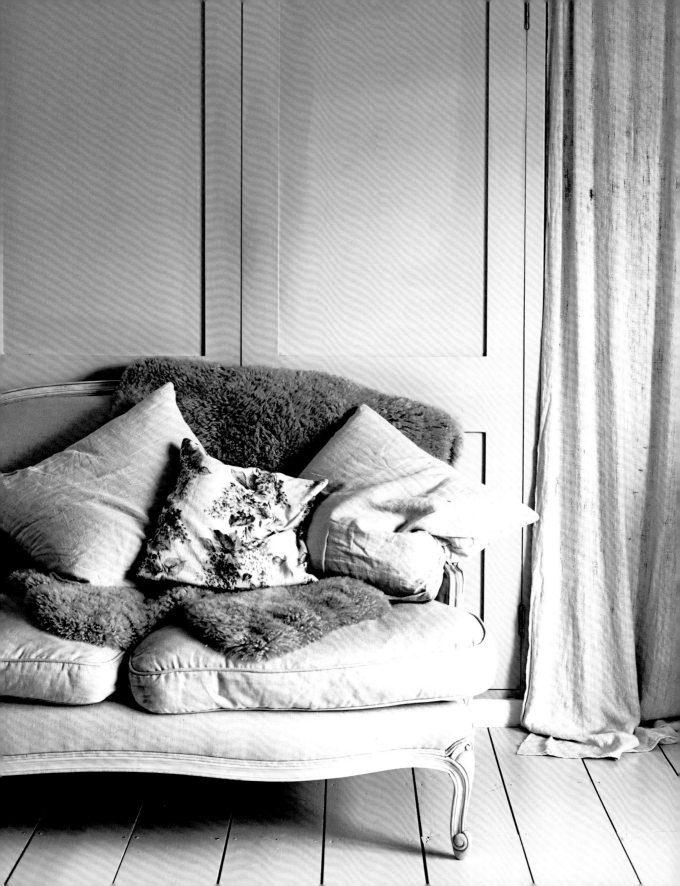

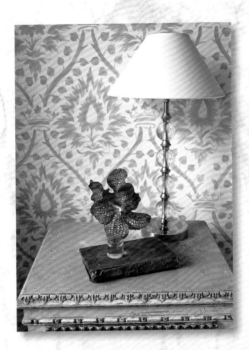

WHY DO WE ALL LOVE GREY?

Back in 2009, I wrote an article for the UK's *Independent* newspaper headlined: 'Grey Paint: Top of the Pots'. Here's what I said: "Whether you're moving or improving, a neutral base is generally a good start and the colour experts at Dulux have decided that grey is the new magnolia, only they are calling it Steel Symphony, because no one actually wants to paint their house grey." (Pause here for mocking laughter as we reflect on just how wrong I was. Because clearly everyone wanted to paint their house grey.) This new trend for grey was, said international paint manufacturer Dulux, part of a trend towards a more sophisticated look with a refined modern twist.

THE PERFECT NEUTRAL

Both interiors experts and paint experts agree that grey is only just beginning to hit the mainstream. You might feel like you've been sitting in grey-painted bars and restaurants for years, but in fact it's only recently that the colour has spread from the walls of interior designers' homes and the pages of magazines to, well, every other house in the street.

So why this passion for grey and where has it come from? There are, perhaps unsurprisingly, as many different answers to this as there are shades of grey (many, many more than 50, by the way). Theories range from the gloom and doom of the current world economic climate to the change in artificial lighting from incandescent bulbs to LEDs, via our new love for all things Nordic and the popularity of grey in fashion.

RIGHT *Grey will change colour according to the natural light in the room, so if you have windows on more than one side, you need to take that into account when choosing your shade. Try Little Greene French Grey for a warm pale grey that won't dominate or darken a space.*

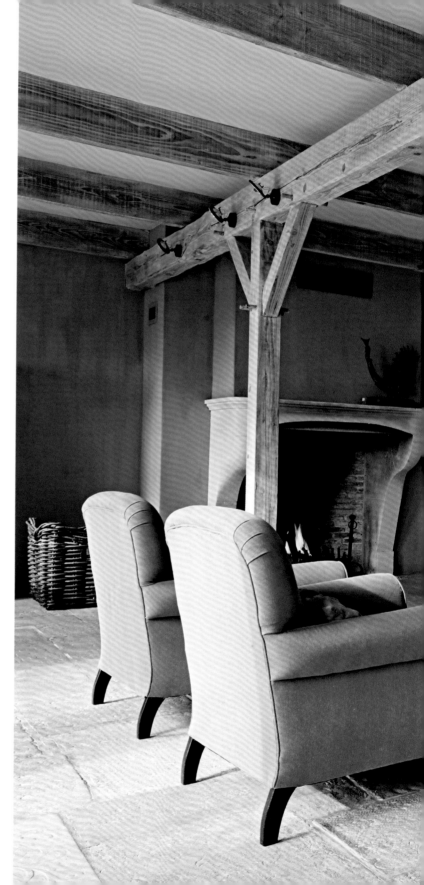

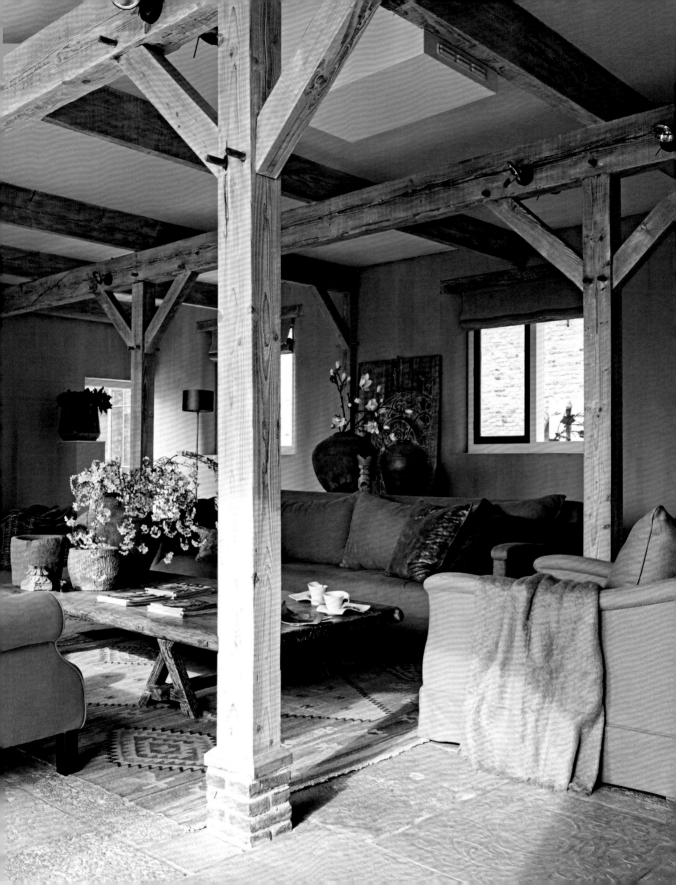

THIS PAGE *Dark grey in a bedroom is really restful; add pale bedlinen in summer and switch to something dark and cosy in winter.*

Fancy that

Of the 28 shades of grey in the Little Greene paint range, only one – Gauze – is made purely from black and white. It is not a bestseller.

According to PPG, the automotive paint firm that supplies most of the industry, 76 per cent of all new cars sold in the UK in 2010 were either grey, silver, black or white.

THIS PAGE *Painting your furniture to match the walls is a great way to create layers of texture and colour.*

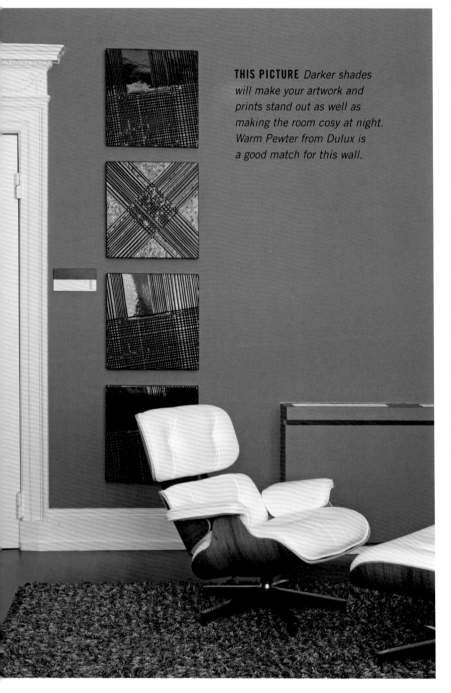

THIS PICTURE *Darker shades will make your artwork and prints stand out as well as making the room cosy at night. Warm Pewter from Dulux is a good match for this wall.*

OPPOSITE TOP LEFT *Mix patterns and textures in different shades of grey to create a warm, tonal effect. This makes it easy to change one or two cushions for a totally different look.*

OPPOSITE TOP RIGHT *A plain grey headboard with white bedlinen is a classic look. Keep it monochrome or add colour with a throw that you can change with the seasons.*

Interior design has always followed fashion – just look at the recent mania for all things 1970s, which started on the catwalk and quickly spread to our houses via cork furniture, macramé plant holders and the return of that 1970s staple, the house plant. Still not convinced? A few seasons ago, Burberry Prorsum sent a jumper with an owl motif down a runway. Within weeks, lifestyle stores were selling owl cushions, candlesticks and cups.

Tony Glenville, the creative director of the School of Media and Communications at the London College of Fashion, says grey has slowly been replacing black on the catwalk for several seasons now. "Although black still sells, it has been slowly eroded by other neutral colours – including brown and navy as well as grey. The use of grey came from a need for a trans-seasonal colour, since fashion now delivers so many times a year. It works as a black substitute, an eco colour and looks great in everything from brocade to cashmere."

OPPOSITE BOTTOM LEFT *Everything has more impact against a grey wall. A floral lamp becomes more modern; a painting more dramatic.*

OPPOSITE BOTTOM RIGHT *Coloured glass vases make a statement against a velvety grey wall. Swap accessories to keep your décor looking fresh.*

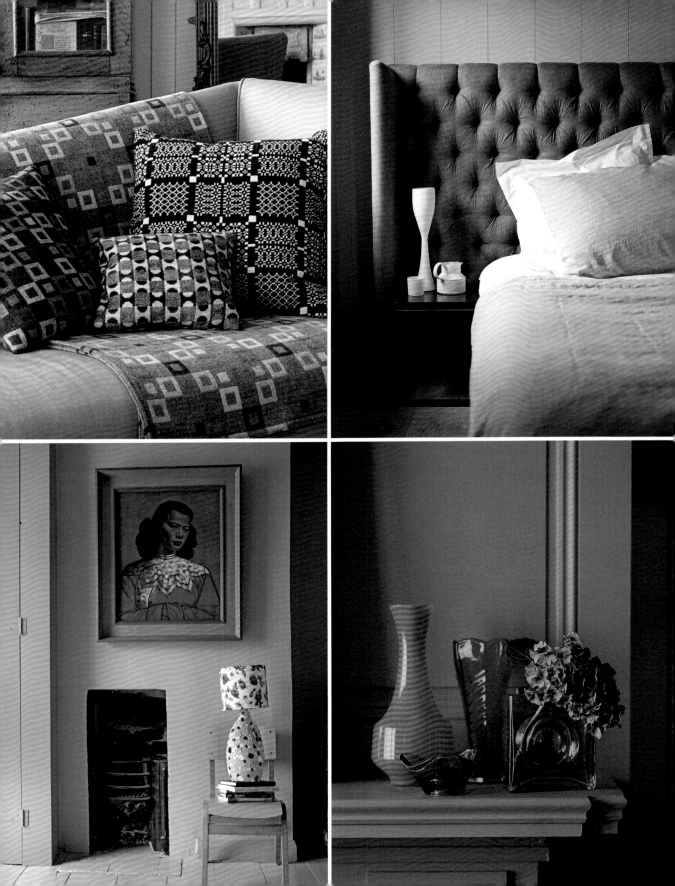

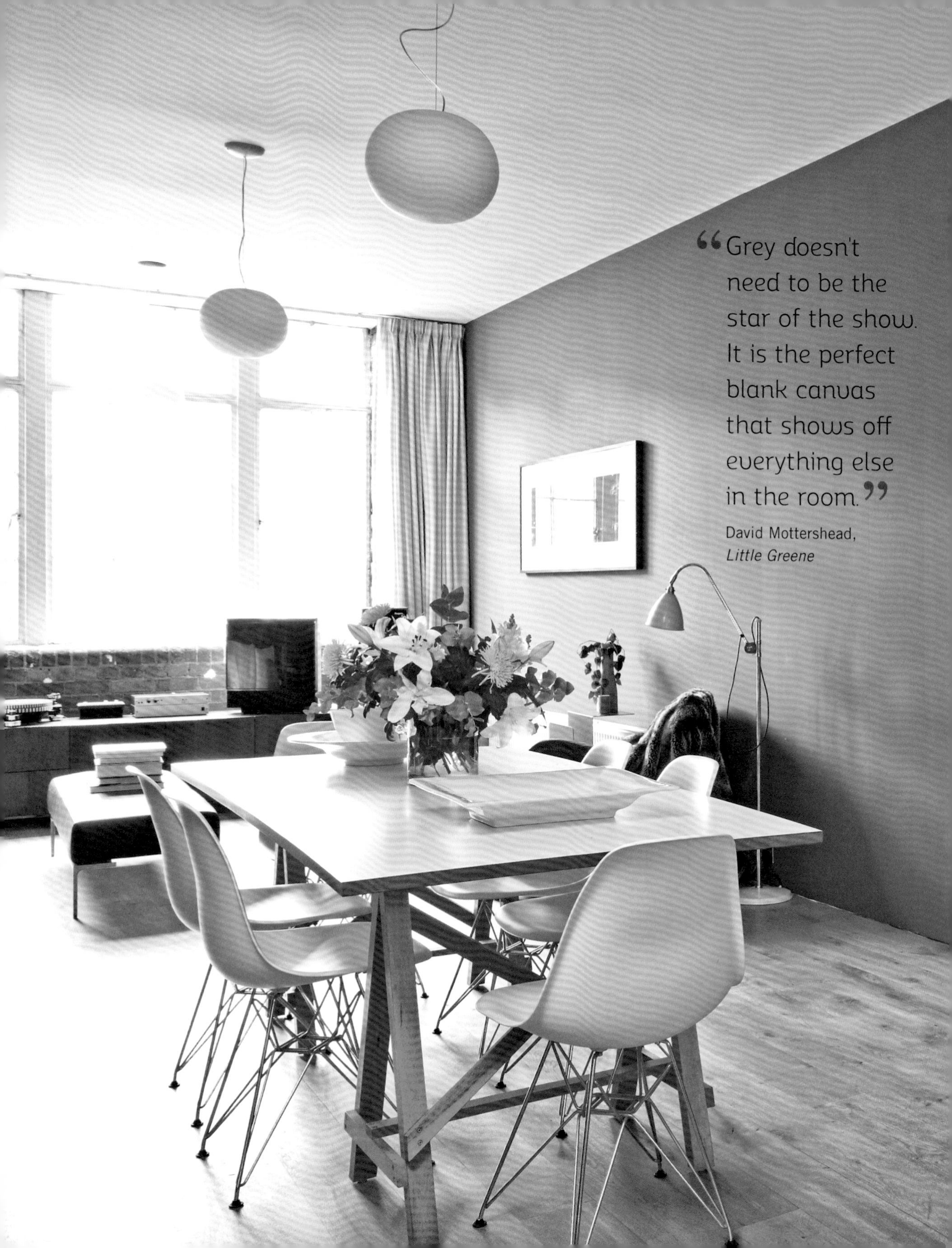

> "Grey doesn't need to be the star of the show. It is the perfect blank canvas that shows off everything else in the room."

David Mottershead,
Little Greene

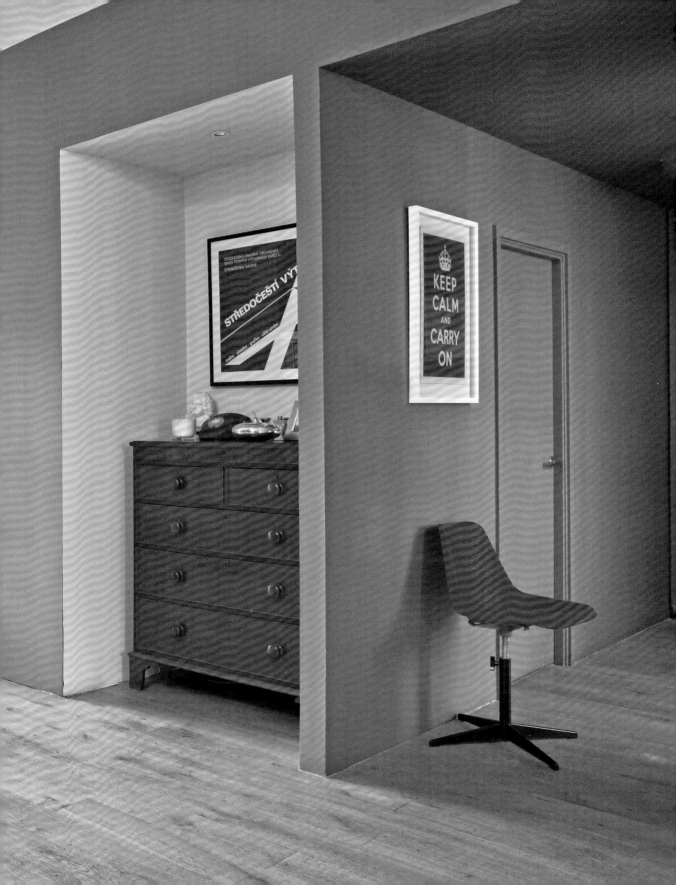

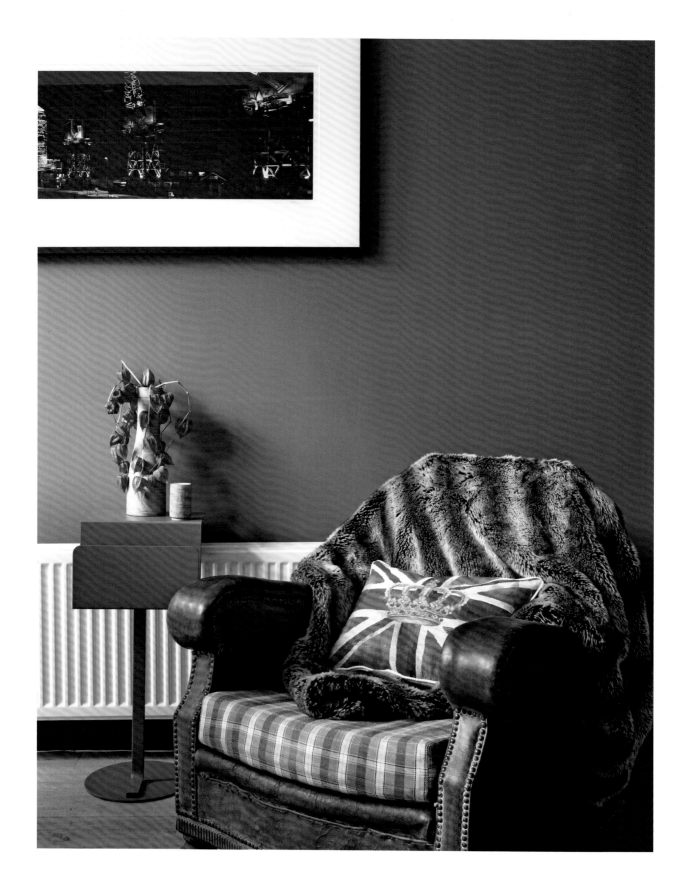

Susie Rumbold, president elect of the British Institute of Interior Design and a former fashion buyer, has often witnessed the spillover of trends from fashion to interiors. "The crossover tends to be in details and accent colours because interiors need to last longer than the average garment. You might buy a jacket in the latest shade of blue and ditch it after a season, but you are unlikely to redecorate your house every year."

Grey can be an accent colour, but more often it is used as a base shade for a scheme with accents of contrasting, fashion-influenced colours layered on top, Susie Rumbold of the British Institute of Interior Design says. "It's universally versatile and easy to live with. Grey has been a dominant trend in UK domestic interiors for the last decade, and I think its enduring popularity is related in part to the cold, clear, northern light we enjoy in this country. Put simply, grey just looks good here."

OPPOSITE *If you're brave enough to go for a dark shade of grey, then I would paint the radiators as well, to make them disappear. This wall is painted in Farrow & Ball Railings, a softer alternative to black.*

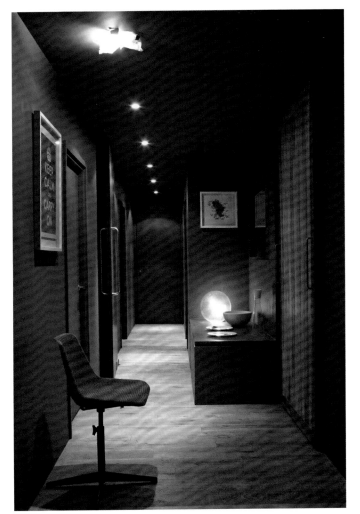

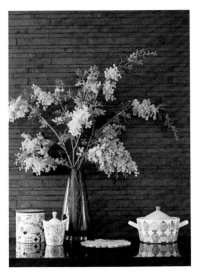

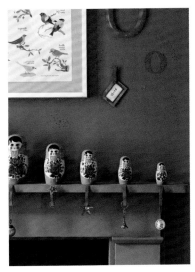

ABOVE *Painting a small space white won't always make it look bigger. Sometimes it will just look like a small white room. Embrace its size and choose a dark colour to add drama.*

FAR LEFT *Using a textured wallpaper will add interest to a plain grey wall.*

LEFT *Grey goes with all the other colours on the wheel, so throw in some pink until you feel like a change and then swap it for orange or yellow. It's more affordable to swap the accessories than the wall colour.*

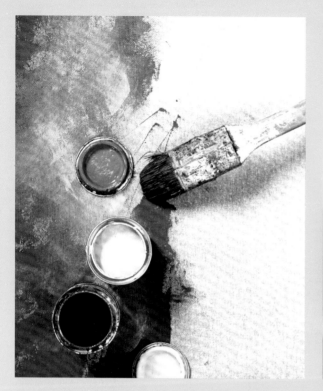

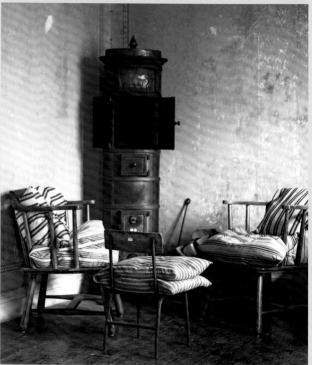

◦~~ Expert opinion ~◦

The celebrated American designer Kelly Wearstler says grey has a mercurial personality. *"It can be masculine or feminine, strong or subtle depending on the execution and overall design palette. Unique colour combinations can create either visual tension or harmony — both of which are equally beautiful. I love playing shades of grey off metallic, marble or handpainted silk wallcoverings within a room. A monochromatic palette allows geometric forms, patterns and textures to have a stronger voice."*

Kelly's favourite greys are from a range by the environmentally friendly Sydney Harbour, a Californian paint company, from which she would choose White Rhino. She also recommends London Fog by Pratt & Lambert.

ABOVE *It might say grey on the tin, but inside it could be anything from vaguely beige to a distinctly blue colour. Grey is the one colour where you will have to invest in sample pots to get it right.*

OPPOSITE *Painting the fireplace in a darker version of the wall colour rather than traditional black gives a room a more contemporary feel and adds a touch of the unexpected.*

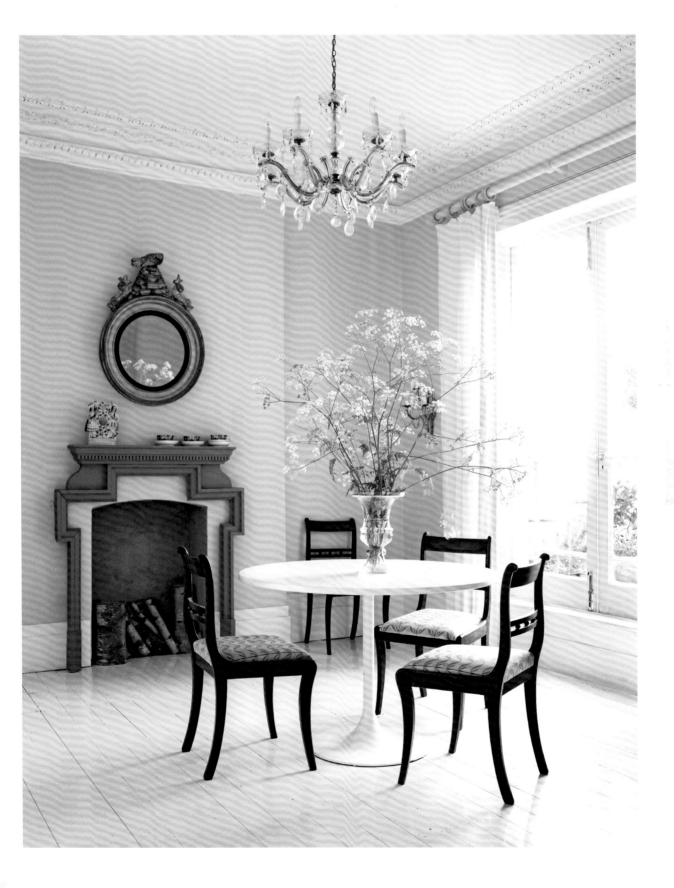

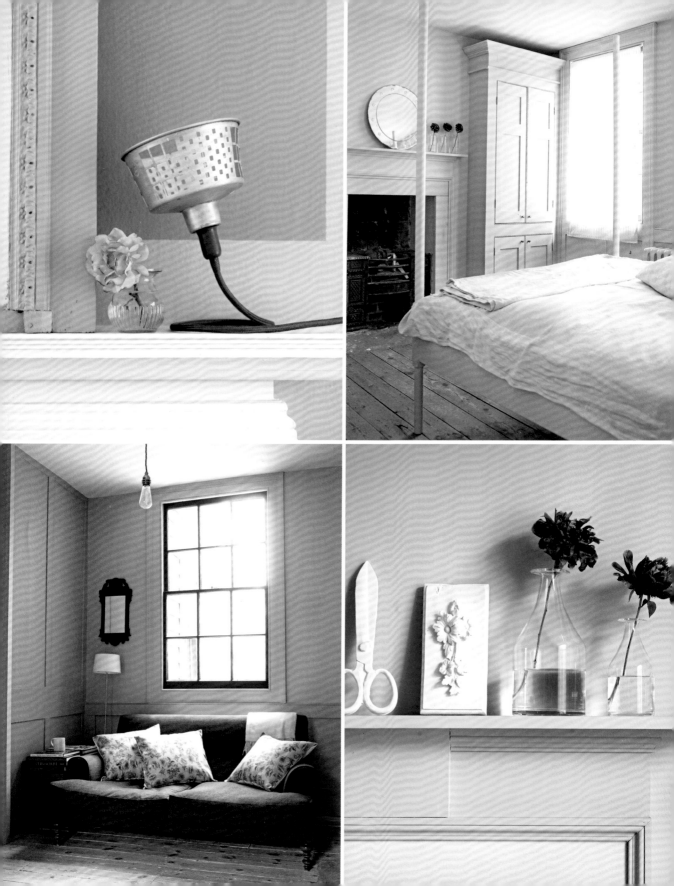

David Mottershead, managing director of The Little Greene Paint Company, says grey is so popular because, once you have found the right shade, it's completely comfortable to live with. "It is almost a non-colour and it acts as the perfect blank canvas for our possessions. It goes with everything and everything looks good against it. It's also much easier to change the furniture in a grey room because so many colours go with it." Which makes grey very practical. Once you've got the right shade, you won't need to redecorate if you buy a new sofa, or re-cover Granny's old armchair.

Another theory why grey is the colour of the decade is that our tastes have been influenced by gritty Nordic TV dramas, which seem to be as avidly followed for their interiors as for finding out whodunnit. My Twitter feed is usually so busy raving about the design classics or the colour of the walls behind the murderer that we are quite likely to miss the thrilling denouement altogether...

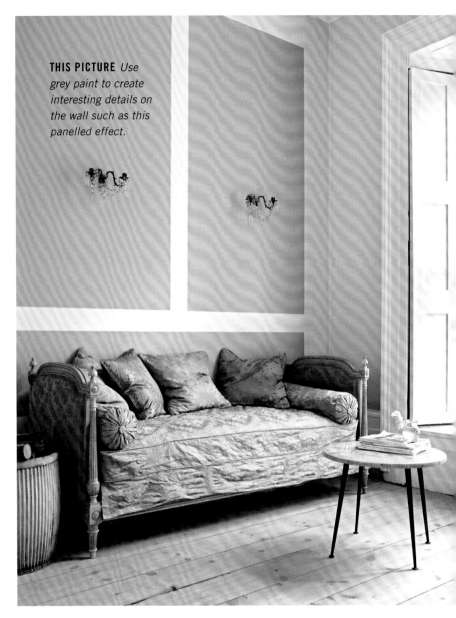

THIS PICTURE *Use grey paint to create interesting details on the wall such as this panelled effect.*

OPPOSITE TOP LEFT *Hardwick White by Farrow & Ball is a perfect neutral with a hint of grey. White woodwork will give a crisp, modern finish.*

OPPOSITE TOP RIGHT *Try using the same colour through the whole house and paint the skirting/base boards and cupboards to match. You can* also paint the ceiling, which will give the impression that it is further away and make your rooms look larger.

OPPOSITE BOTTOM LEFT *Sticking to one colour throughout your home will maximize the sense of space and, as the light will change from room to room, will keep the spaces looking* alive. The colour will also vary according to the time of day.

OPPOSITE BOTTOM RIGHT *Pale grey is the perfect backdrop to white accessories and makes a room look both lighter and brighter than white, which, in a dark room, can have a dull rather than a dramatic effect.*

Fancy that

The French term 'Grisette' referred to young working class women – girls who wore drab grey dresses, perhaps because they were supposed to be invisible and to blend into the background.

THIS PAGE *Try Dulux Night Jewels 1 for a strong charcoal colour that gives a really intense finish.*

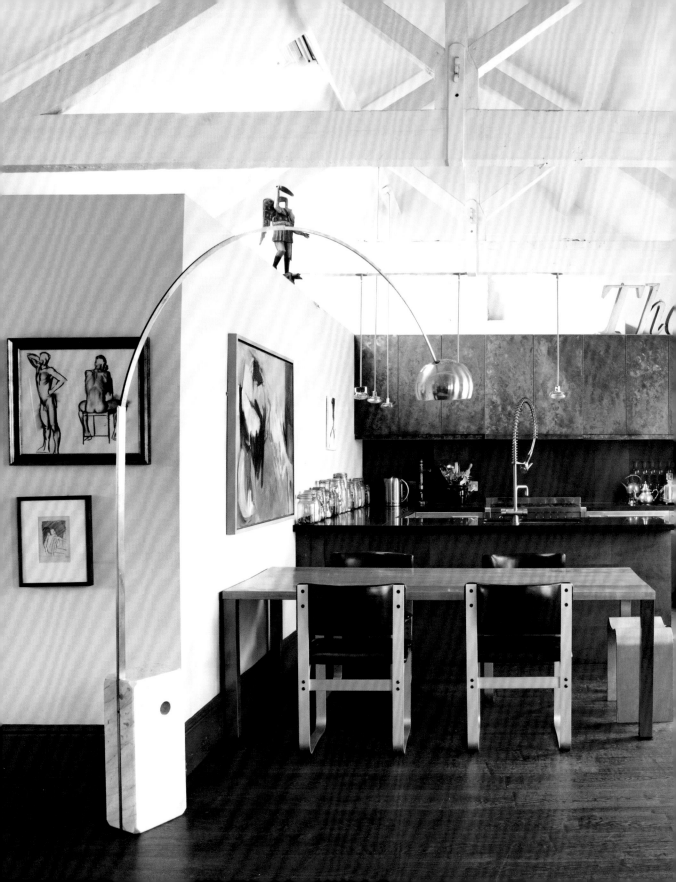

This loft apartment is painted in Chemise, an archived Farrow & Ball colour, but French Grey by Little Greene is a good alternative. It's a warm grey that goes with pretty much everything and is often my standard recommendation for people who want a warm shade of grey that isn't too dominant.

WHO MURDERED MAGNOLIA?

This is a bit of whodunnit. An interior designer's murder mystery. Did grey kill magnolia? Well, I can exclusively reveal that grey is innocent. It was the light bulb all along!

Often derided as 'builder's beige', poor old magnolia was, for many years, the go-to paint colour for landlords, developers and those who just didn't care about or notice their surroundings. It has become a byword for all that is bland, blah and boring in interiors. This inoffensive neutral has managed to simultaneously become both the most ubiquitous and the most disliked shade on the domestic paint chart. For a neutral, it provokes a fairly un-neutral reaction.

Yet, ironically, magnolia's neutrality and practicality (it won't show the dirt and has a warm, peachy base, so doesn't discolour like other pale shades) is precisely what everyone now dislikes about it. But how did magnolia go from being top of the (paint) charts in the 1970s and '80s to Public Enemy Number One just a few years later? Well, it was Ikea. Not content with urging us to chuck out our chintz, they had to murder magnolia as well.

THIS PAGE *While many think of grey as a modern, urban colour better suited to the city, it works perfectly in traditional more rural settings too. An antique bench and old wooden table will instantly look more contemporary set against a pale grey wall.*

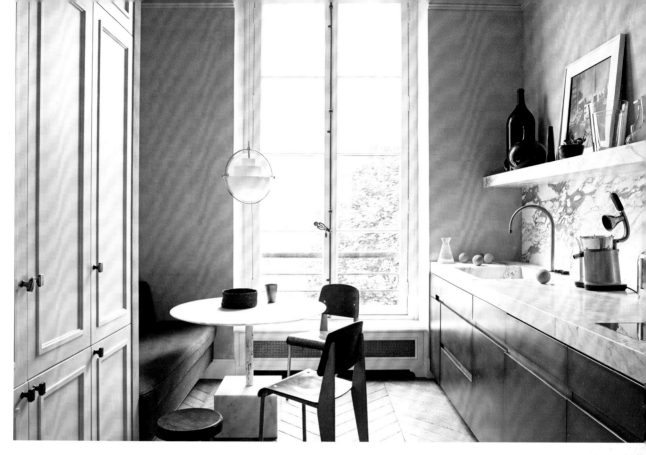

ABOVE *Introduce some contemporary touches to a grey kitchen with a marble splashback and classic design chairs.*

RIGHT *A classic sofa will instantly look more modern when set against a dark grey wall, and a pot of paint is a much more affordable update than new furniture.*

Here's the thing: in the blueish light of the northern hemisphere, rooms can look cold during the daytime. Cover the walls in white paint and the result can be postively chilly. So, back in the last century, householders consciously chose to paint their homes in warm shades. (Yes, that's why the 1970s are brown and orange in all the photographs.)

Then they added soft reds, sunshiny yellows and lots and lots of natural wood. And magnolia was the perfect rich, creamy, complementary shade to suggest a feeling of warm homeliness.

At night, we switched on the electric light – those old tungsten bulbs, which give off a warm, yellow glow akin to candlelight. And, just as candles are flattering to a complexion, magnolia paint loved those bulbs. Its soft, warming tones turned chilly rooms into cosy havens of relaxation and comfort.

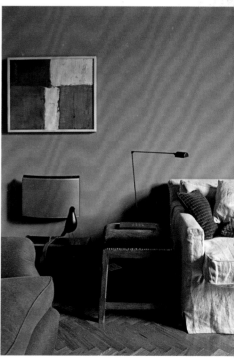

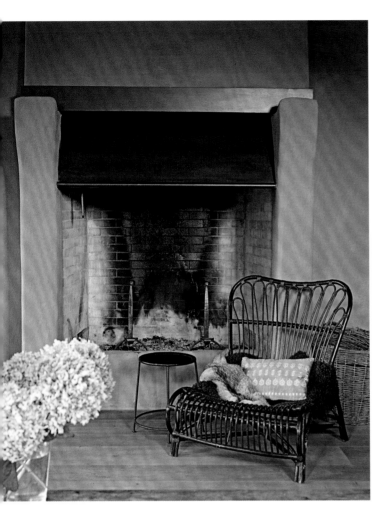

The years passed, and magnolia continued to work well with the black and chrome trends of the 1980s, as it warmed up (and even offset) the harsh colours and materials so popular in that decade. But then everything changed. As the incandescent bulb uses more energy, it was deemed to be environmentally damaging and in came halogen, LED and compact fluorescent lamps, with their harsher, cooler, clearer light. In the blink of an eye, magnolia looked terrible.

"Magnolia is a sort of stony cream that worked beautifully with the old incandescent bulbs," says Marianne Shillingford, the creative director of Dulux. "And it looked absolutely ghastly under the glare from a compact fluorescent light. Really, truly horrible."

But what's that got to do with Ikea? Well, when the first halogen bulbs came along, they were prohibitively expensive and the preserve of interior designers with wealthy clients. But thanks to Ikea's vast buying power, it could manufacture and sell halogens cheaply. So it did. The joy of halogen is that it casts a clear, sharp light. Which works brilliantly with greys and monochromes, but is a disaster for warm, creamy white. Poor old magnolia never stood a chance.

THIS PAGE AND OPPOSITE *Grey is the most versatile colour for decorating; not just because there are so many shades, but also because it can change its personality according to what you put with it. It will sit happily with rustic wood tables or sleek chrome lights, chunky knitted cushions and casual furniture. Whether you choose to keep a simple monochrome palette for dramatic impact or prefer to surround yourself with a rainbow of colours, grey will set them all off perfectly.*

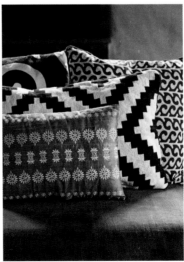

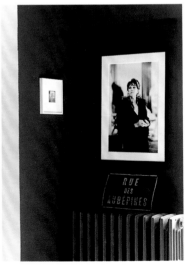

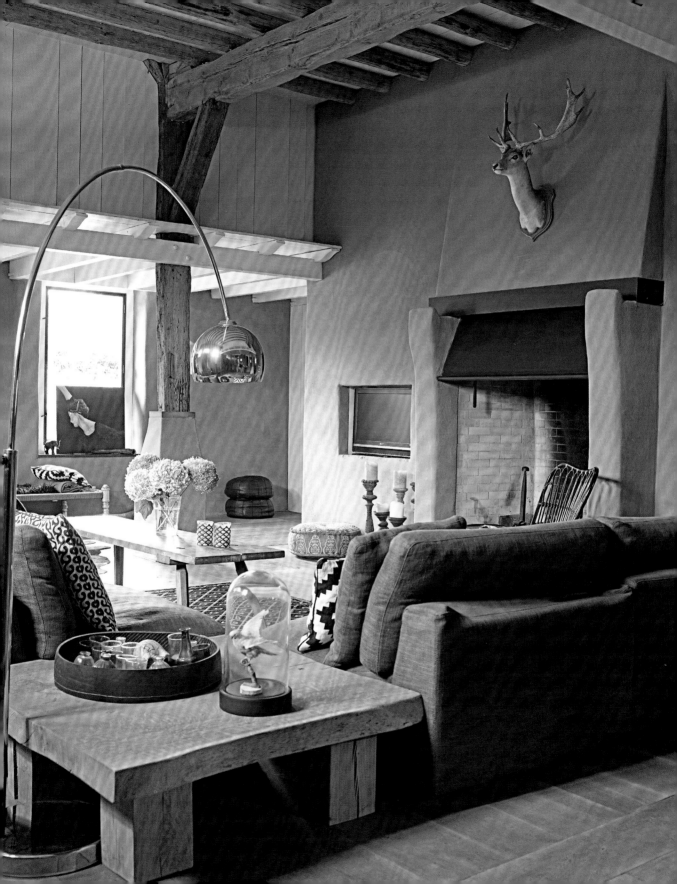

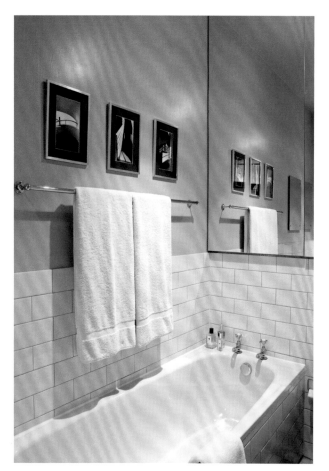

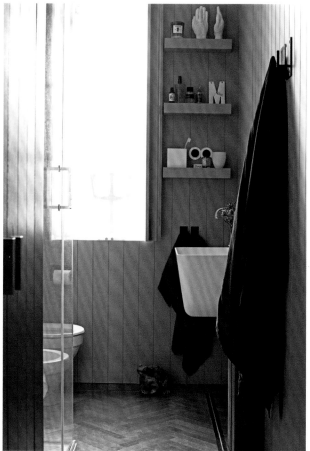

ABOVE LEFT *A mid-grey above the classic subway tile brings a clean, contemporary look to this bathroom, while darker-painted tongue and groove would be warmer and more rustic.*

ABOVE RIGHT *For some reason, grey hasn't traditionally been used much in bathrooms, but it can look fabulous against the white sanitaryware and can be both ultra modern or comfortably traditional.*

Most of us never even saw it coming. To me, like everyone else, tastes seemed to be changing. We thought we were simply moving towards more modern colours and shades. We didn't understand, argues Marianne Shillingford, that it wasn't our changing tastes but the changing light. But, she says, there is some hope for magnolia. Lighting is undergoing huge changes. LEDs are poised to take over from compact fluorescents and designers are starting to create warm, white light that will once again flatter poor old neglected magnolia. But, just as halogen was once out of the reach of most of us, so LEDs remain expensive.

Until Ikea waved its mighty wand. The store now stocks a range of warm – and affordable – LED lights. So, if you live in a magnolia-painted flat, there is hope. First, you can either change the bulbs to warm LEDs, or turn to tungsten filament bulbs (screamingly fashionable and eyewateringly expensive) to warm up your walls. You could even pair them with other yellow-based shades, such as warm blues and greens, to warm things up a bit.

Or you can simply sit tight and wait for magnolia to come back into fashion. According to Marianne Shillingford, it may take a generation but – just like Arnold Schwarzenegger – it will be back...

THIS PAGE *Sticking to two colours in the bedroom makes for a restful and calming space. It doesn't matter if you prefer pale grey for light mornings or dark for a more cocooning cosy space, just keep the bedlinen white and it will always look fresh and welcoming, classic yet contemporary.*

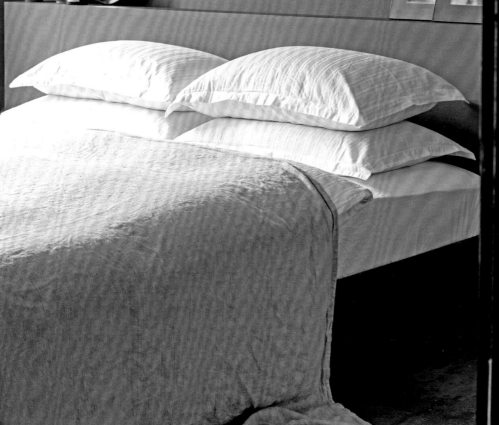

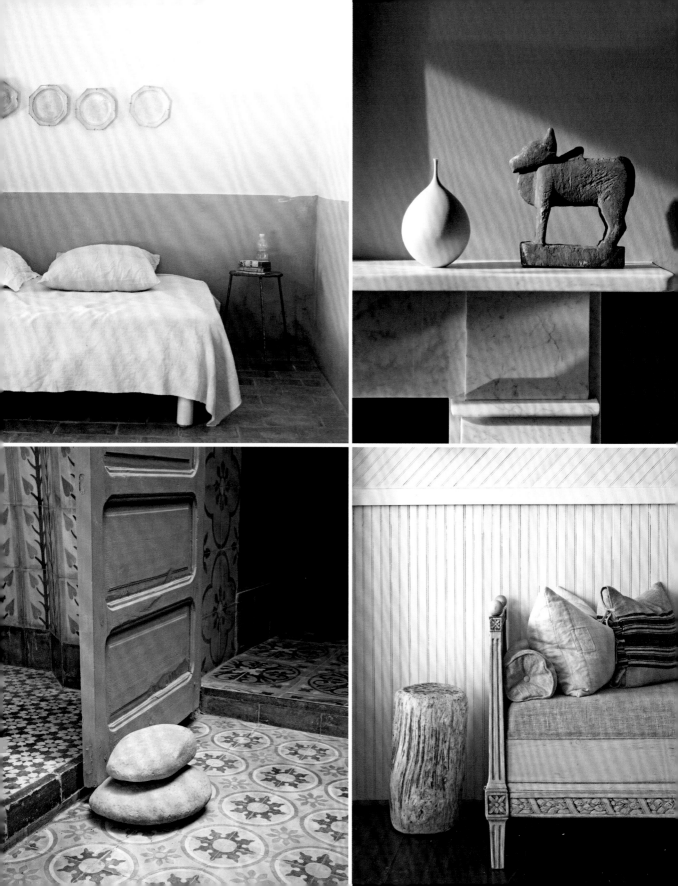

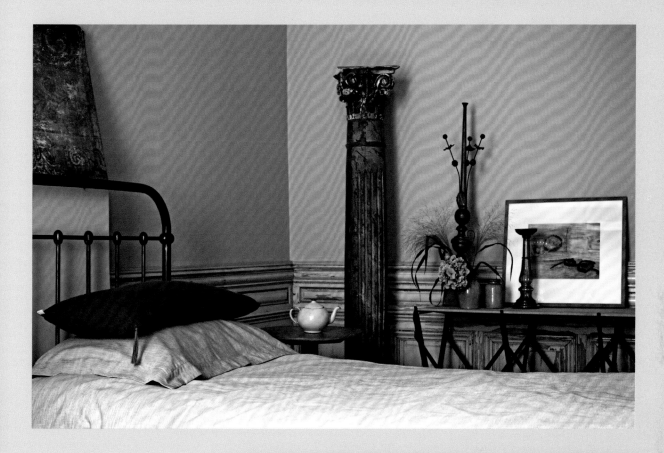

OPPOSITE AND ABOVE *Whether you want to paint half the wall, either top or bottom or the whole thing from floor to ceiling, cover the doors or add it to the woodwork, there is a shade of grey that is just perfect for your house. All you have to do is track it down. Remember that shadows will make the room darker, so do take angles, alcoves, corners and windows into account when choosing.*

Expert opinion

Sophie Paterson, a luxury interior designer based in Surrey, England, uses a lot of grey in her contemporary classic interiors. She says *"My favourite brand is Zoffany, as the colours are very reliable. My go-to grey is Paris Grey – it's warm with a slight green undertone, which looks great with almost any colour scheme, although you should avoid pairing it with purple, as that brings out the green too much. I also love Silver, Silver-Double and Silver-Half, which is a very true grey with a slight blue undertone and that stays consistent with different lighting."* When it comes to tester pots, Sophie says you must paint directly onto at least two walls. *"It might seem like a hassle, but it will avoid time-consuming and costly errors."*

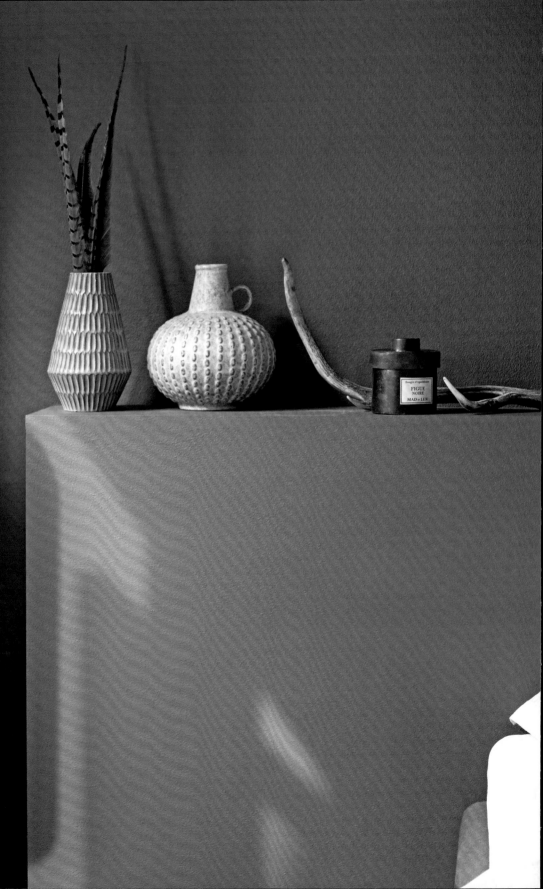

"Human nature is not black and white but black and grey."
Graham Greene

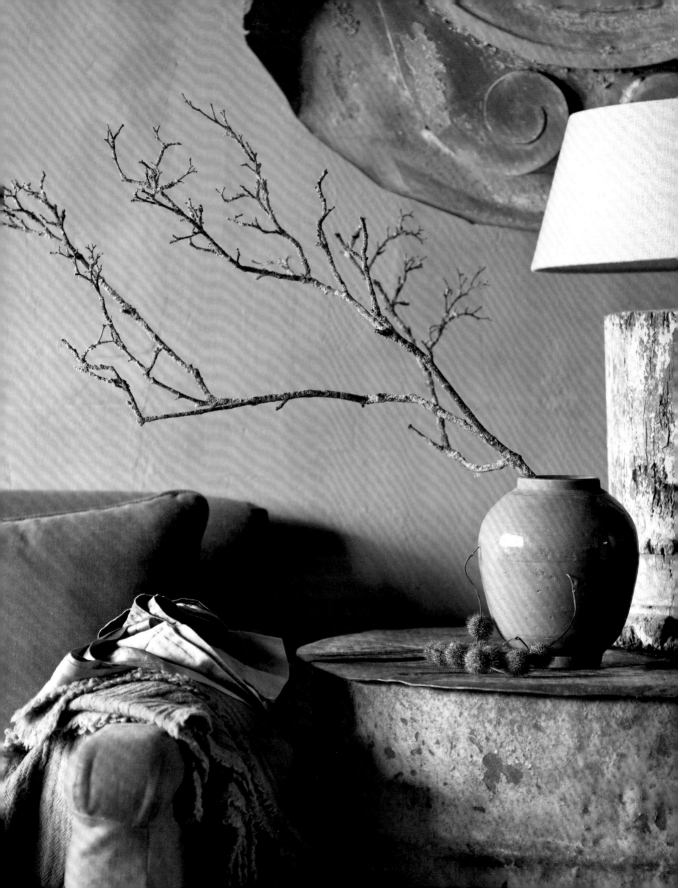

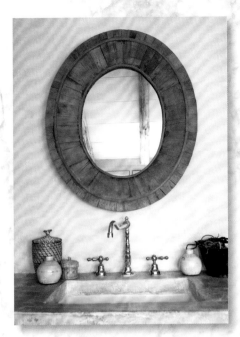

THE PSYCHOLOGY OF GREY

Many people argue that grey has become popular because it fits perfectly with our current mood. Economic woes, financial crises, austerity programmes and uncertainty about the future all contribute to a grey feeling. Pure grey (and we're talking a simple mix of black and white here) has some negative connotations: boredom, indecision, indifference and old age. So why is it that grey has become the colour du jour when it comes to interiors?

WHEN GREY MAKES YOU FEEL BLUE

Karen Haller, a leading applied colour psychology expert, says grey is a fascinating colour. "You never hear anyone say 'Oh, I love it when the sky is grey', so why do so many people choose to live in grey?" she asks. "I feel it has something to do with shutting out modern-day life and our need to hide away."

Karen continues, "The current trend to paint bedrooms pure grey has resulted in SOS calls from people asking why they are feeling so tired and drained. That's the grey sapping their energy, so that instead of waking up feeling energized they are reaching for a double espresso."

Karen, whose own house is decorated in warm, earthy tones, says pure grey is the only colour with no direct positive psychological properties. She goes even further: "Grey can convey both indecision and a lack of confidence. It's the colour you wear when you don't want to be seen, when you want to hide your personality, so it's like cocooning yourself from the outside world."

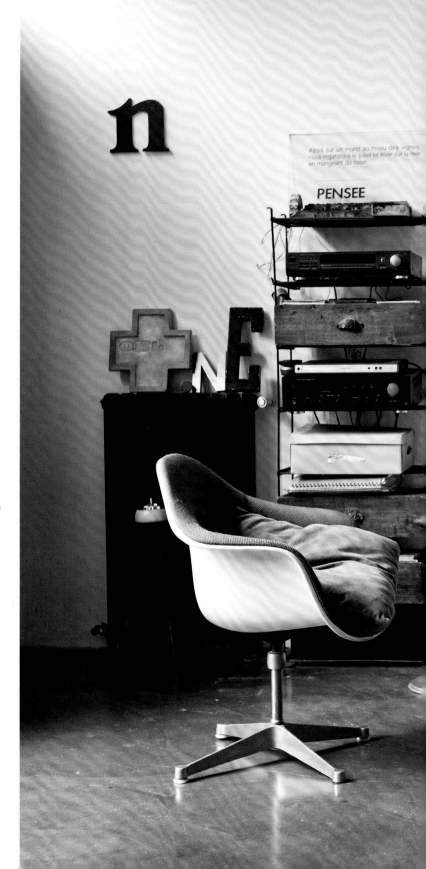

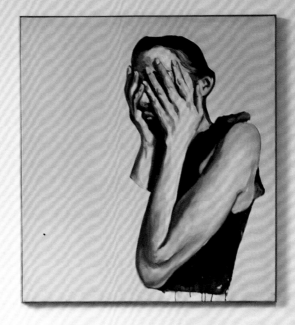

THIS PAGE *A grey concrete floor could look stark and cold, but paired with rustic woods and layered textiles, it creates a comfortable and inviting space. Try Benjamin Moore's Ally's Earring, inspired by an antique pearl, for a soft grey shade that won't be cold and which will soften industrial pieces.*

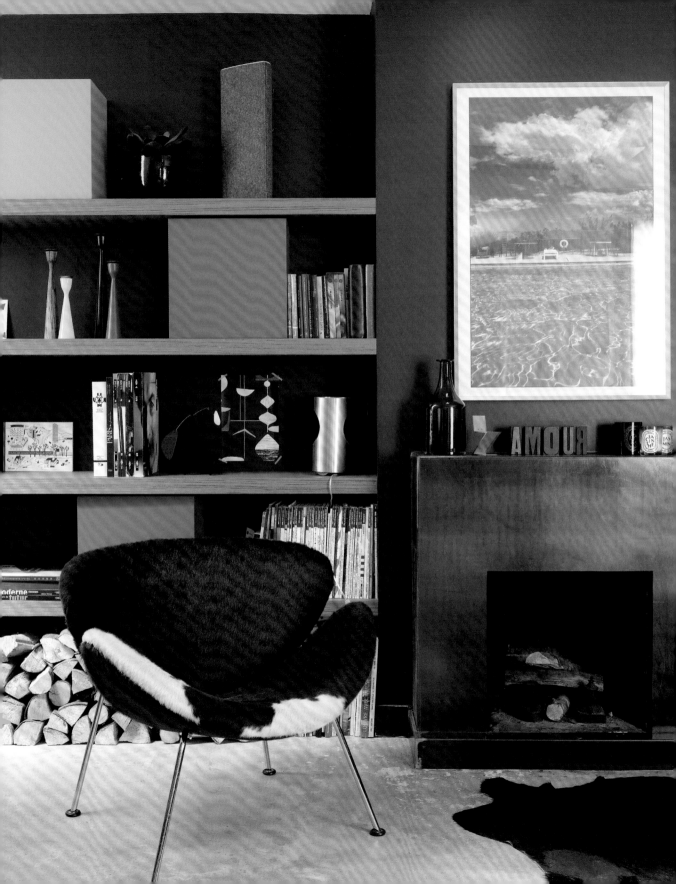

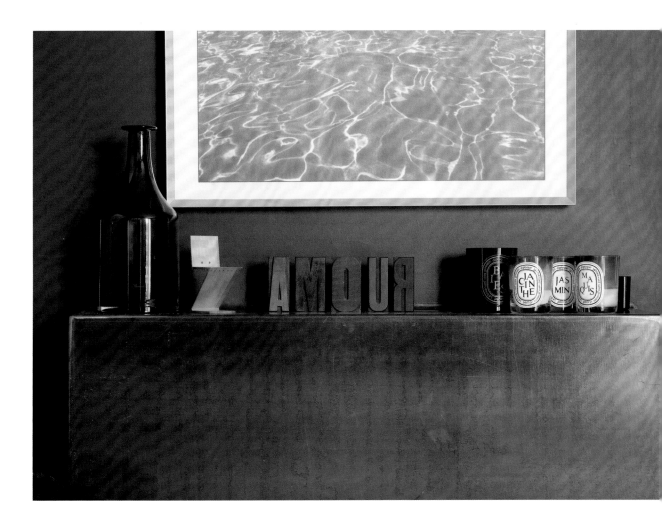

When it comes to using grey in our homes, Karen recommends that it shouldn't be applied to bedrooms, children's rooms or any rooms where you might exercise your creativity. So that rules out the kitchen, the dining room that doubles up as an office and, for some of us, the bathroom. And leaves us with a small corner of the sitting room. TV personality and designer Laurence Llewelyn-Bowen claims you shouldn't put grey anywhere you are planning on having sex, as it's a passion killer, but I'll leave you to decide which rooms that rules out.

Leatrice Eiseman, an American colour specialist and executive director of the Pantone Color Institute, agrees with Karen. "Everything about colour depends on context. In an area where there is not much sunlight, grey is repeating the greyness in the atmosphere, so for people who are prone to depression on overcast days, this is not a good choice." She continues, "If grey feels very natural and comfortable to you, then use it, but if you are choosing it because it is a trend or someone has advised you, you will never really feel at home with it."

OPPOSITE AND ABOVE
Go as dark as you dare for maximum impact. In this room, the pops of teal and turquoise lighten the room and the cowhide chair brings warmth to what might otherwise be an oppressive space. Always include some natural wood in a scheme, whatever shade of grey you are using.

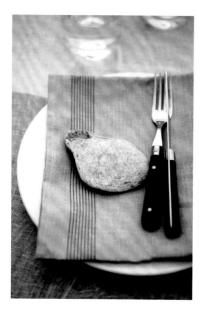

LEFT *Traditional crockery and linen napkins look more modern and dramatic when set on a grey place mat.*

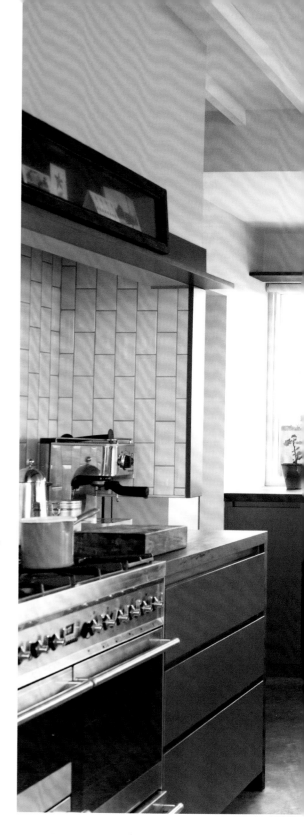

For those of you who are unconvinced by all this, I offer up my own personal experience. Not as an expert of colour psychology, but merely as a lover of grey paint.

My sitting room is painted a very dark shade of grey – Down Pipe by Farrow & Ball, a colour that was originally designed for guttering because it disguises pipes against brickwork. However, it looks great with a pink sofa in front of it too. And a dark grey velvet one. I have a black cloakroom and grey bookshelves, there is a dark grey wall in the spare room and a black carpet in another.

Anyway, back to the cautionary tale. I recently painted my north-facing kitchen a beautiful shade of pale grey. I did this against all the advice. The experts told me it wouldn't work in a north-facing room. "Rubbish!" I thought. "I know better." And indeed, it was great… at first. In certain lights it was warm and inviting. In others, it was, I have to admit, cold and dreary. I work at the kitchen table and I began to feel that I wasn't being productive. I just didn't like being there as much. So when my husband, taking his life into his hands, suggested that the room wasn't working and we should redecorate, I agreed with him. Much to our surprise. It was repainted in a chalky shade of white, which works brilliantly with the charcoal shelves and the stainless steel worktop. And I am sitting there now writing this book.

THIS PAGE *The owners of this kitchen have used dark grey on the lower cabinets and chosen a paler shade for the walls and ceiling, which perfectly frames the view outside and makes it seem like it's part of the décor. Pops of mustard yellow and turquoise stand out against the dark grey and create a series of mini still lifes in this working space.*

BREAD

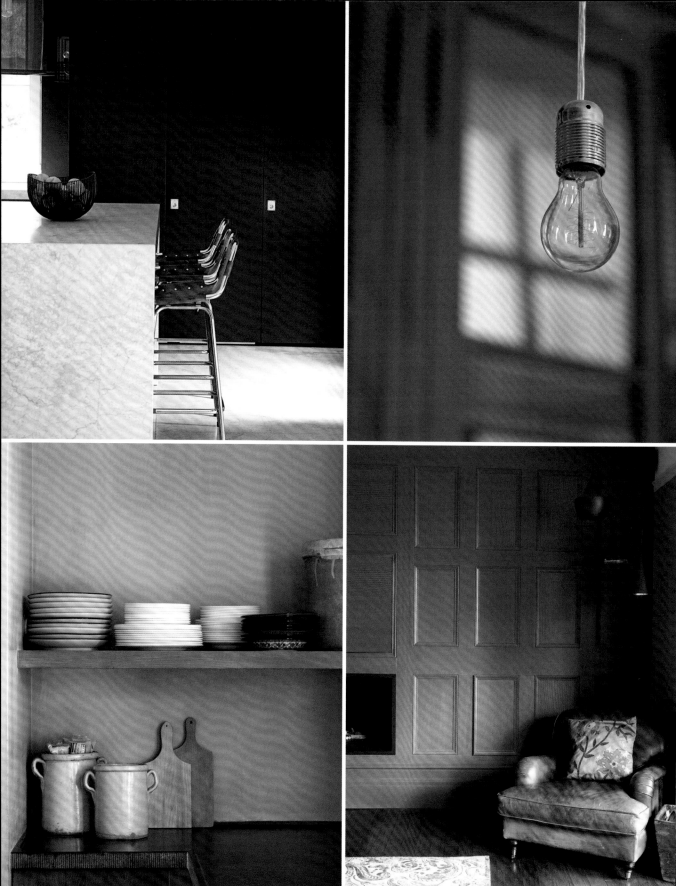

Expert opinion

Emily Henderson, the US interiors stylist and TV presenter, loves grey because *"It's nuanced. It's both masculine and feminine. It's thought-provoking, intellectual and yet totally simple. But paint colours are incredibly tricky, and I'm not an expert on picking the perfect colour the first time AT ALL. I have made some mistakes and learned a few things.*

For instance, what looks good in a picture can look different in the tin, different on your walls, different at night and then different when a blue sofa is placed next to it. It can be 100 per cent baffling. I'm sure if I had gone to art school I would be better at it but I didn't, so it was a lot of trial and error, and I'm finally getting the hang of it.

It's a lot like finding the right guy. Some are great to party with, some are perfect for your family, some just feel like 'home'. Some make you look really good when you are next to them, and some you have a super-unhealthy addiction to and you really don't want to see them anymore but you can't help the attraction and you try again and again to make it work and then you swear them off forever but end up trying them out again only to be disappointed AGAIN. This is me with teal. I am always attracted to it, but I can't seem to actually live with it on my own walls."

Emily's favourites are from upscale US paint company Benjamin Moore. She particularly recommends Gray Owl: *"Super-classic and sophisticated but not boring. A warm grey."* and Oystershell: *"A happy, light, soothing, calming and fresh neutral."* Emily also likes Farrow & Ball's Lamp Room Gray: *"More sophisticated than the other two – and a bit moodier. It's not playful or fun, but more dramatic and sophisticated."*

OPPOSITE *True black can be harsh in a domestic setting but try either Farrow & Ball's Railings or Little Greene's Basalt for a softer shade. Add natural leather, vintage light fittings and rustic accessories for a look that is both dramatic and welcoming. Alternatively, Urban Obsession by Dulux works just as well in a more rural setting and contrasts beautifully with a flowery sofa or cushions.*

RIGHT *Hanging lots of mirrors on a grey wall will immediately bring more light into the room.*

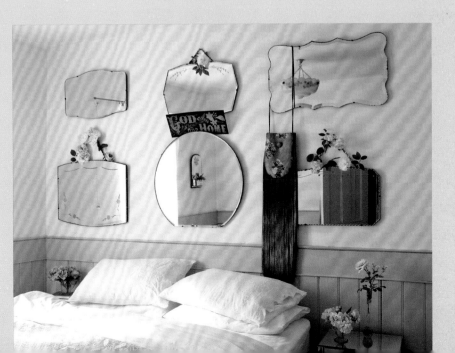

THIS PAGE *By adding flowing curtains and a tablecloth, this monochrome scheme is given a sense of warmth that it might otherwise lack.*

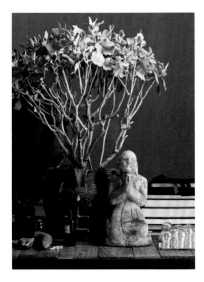

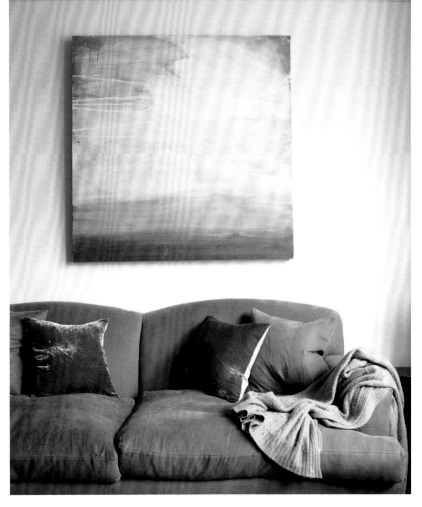

ABOVE *House plants are having a revival after being lost in the design wilderness during the 1980s, and a generous dollop of living green always looks good against a grey wall, whatever the shade.*

RIGHT *If you are worried that grey is a harsh colour, then confound expectations by using it in rich textiles such as velvet, cashmere and faux fur.*

HERE COMES THE SCIENCE BIT

The concept of colour theory could fill a whole book in itself, so let's keep it simple. The colour wheel is the basis from which everything stems. There are three primary colours – red, yellow and blue – and three secondaries – green, violet and orange. But that's not all. In between are six tertiary colours.

The tertiaries break down further – a colour with added white becomes a tint. Add black for a shade, and grey for a tone. They are all based on either yellow or blue. And finally, you need to consider the hue, i.e. the position on the colour wheel and the saturation, meaning a colour's depth and richness, and its brightness.

In 1928 a discovery was made that was fundamental to the way we see colour: of the 16 million colours that the human eye is capable of detecting, it was found that all the different shades stem from how much blue or yellow pigment they contain. That's all it is. There are eight million colours in each spectrum and the main rule is that you can't mix the two.

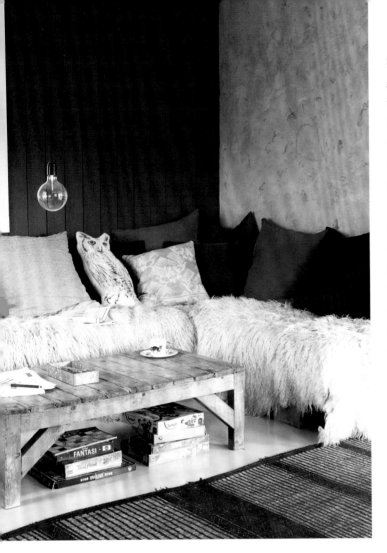

So far, so simple. But 16 million is a lot of colours, and get it wrong by just a few tones and the whole scheme will clash. It's like adding the wrong spice to a meal. If you have ever tried to layer shades of grey and the result has been a soul-sapping muddle, I suggest it's because you have mixed a pink-based grey with a yellow-based one and they are fighting.

You can layer shades of grey, but it's tricky. I prefer to use one strong grey and balance it with a chalky white or even black. Otherwise, you run the risk that it will just look like you couldn't make your mind up. You gotta commit, as they say. Pick a colour and go with it. Light or dark, it doesn't matter... just make the decision. If you do want to use lots of shades of grey, then pick one for the walls and another for the textiles. They're less likely to have an argument that way; pale silk, charcoal knit, fake fur and soft grey linen.

OPPOSITE *This might look like something you would see in a magazine rather than a real home, but use it as inspiration and try painting each door on a row of fitted closets in different shades from the same colour card to create a gentle ombré effect.*

ABOVE *Mixing different greys can be problematic if they don't have the same base notes, but it's a look that's easier to achieve if you mix up your materials: a wood-panelled wall with marble-effect paper and layers of textiles and textures.*

RIGHT *I make it a rule to always include a little black in every room; this helps to anchor the space and give a little dynamic edge to a scheme. Dark grey works perfectly too, from a whole wall to a couple of cushions and a simple lampshade.*

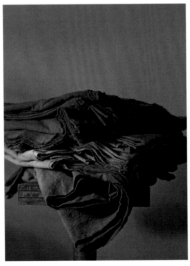

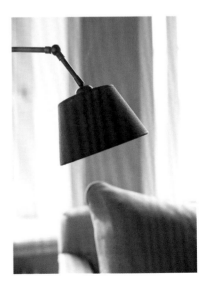

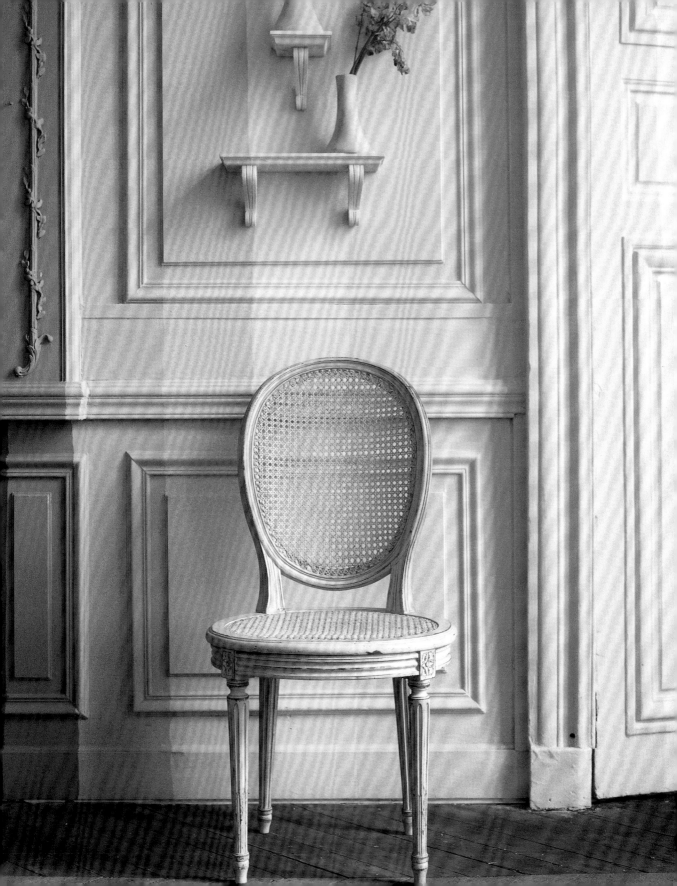

Fancy that

Benjamin Moore has a paint that it claims will remain constant during the changing light, or what it calls 'rise and fall' of the day. Its name? Wall Street. Or what about Perspective? A light grey or a faint blue? It might even be a silver white. It all depends how you look at it.

According to a survey cited on greyorgray.com (yes, there's an actual whole website on this), respondents in both the UK and the US feel that grey is a colour, while gray is a sliding scale of values from black to white.

A LITTLE BIT OF HISTORY

For centuries grey has been regarded as a workmanlike, utilitarian non-colour. The shade of prisons and battleships; items that either don't need to be a more interesting colour, or things that are waiting to be painted. Grey is what we had before colour arrived – think of television and photography. It's also supremely practical as it doesn't show the dirt easily, making it perfect for public spaces.

Back in the Middle Ages, grey was considered a colour for the poor. Sumptuary laws were introduced to regulate the dress of various different classes and only wealthy folk, royalty and members of the aristocracy or the court wore rich, jewel-like shades of red and purple. Monks wore grey – the colour of undyed wool, it symbolized humility and poverty.

Dyes were very expensive until the middle of the 19th century, so grey was a cheap colour and remained so right up to the 20th century. Those who could afford to have their portraits painted wore their brightest clothes, as grey would not have conveyed their wealth and importance.

RIGHT *This room perfectly combines my design rules as explained on the previous pages. Dark grey on the sideboard (Down Pipe by Farrow & Ball) anchors the room with lots of natural wood, and the bricks around the fireplace give this room a welcoming homely feel. For a similar wall colour, try Putty by Dulux or RAL 7044 Silk Grey.*

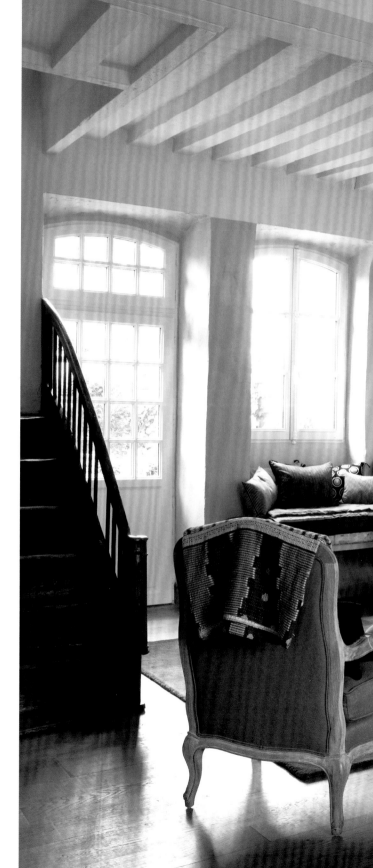

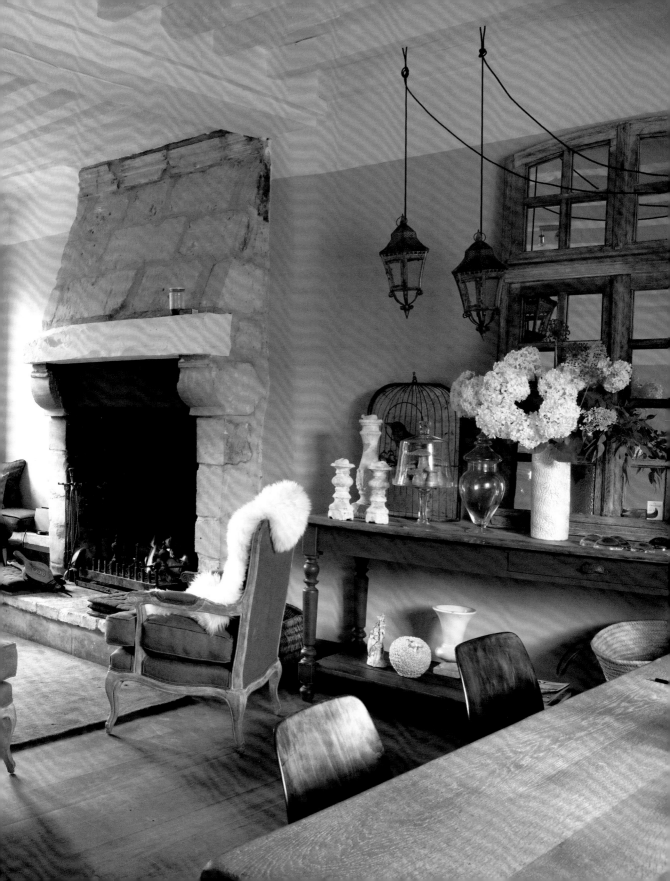

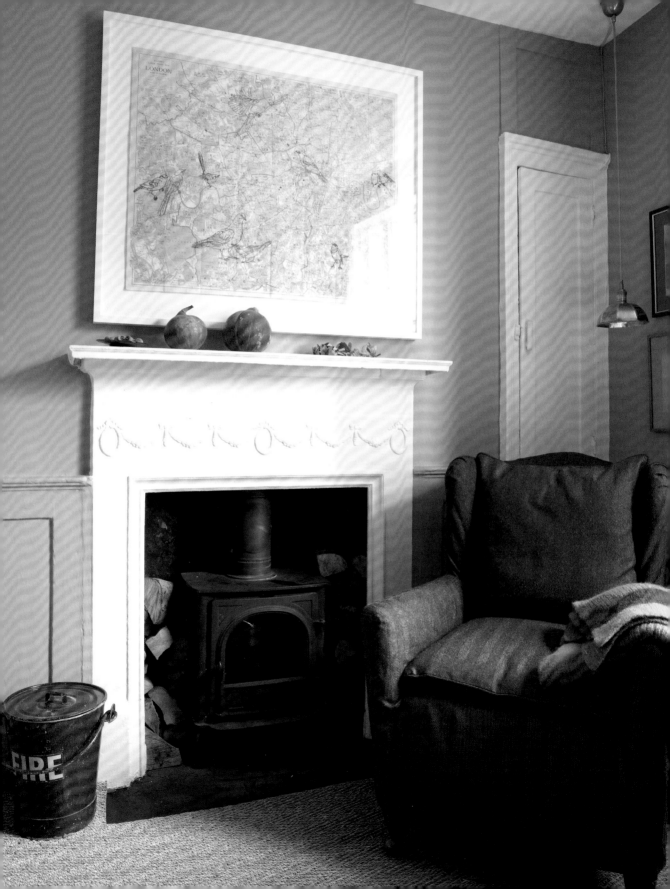

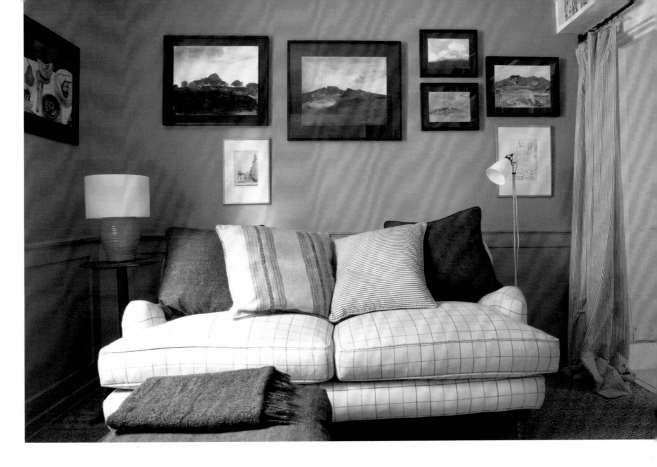

OPPOSITE AND ABOVE

These rooms perfectly illustrate the capricious nature of painting with grey. This is Pigeon by Farrow & Ball and here it has a distinct pale green tinge to it. I have also seen it in a bedroom looking very dark and moody. Two things are certain: it looks great paired with white, and I've never seen an actual pigeon this colour. You will need a tester pot.

Black first became chic in the 1920s, says Tony Glenville, creative director of the School of Media and Communications at the London College of Fashion. Before that, it was only worn as evening dress in expensive, opulent fabrics – think of Sargent's 1884 portrait of *Madame X*, depicting a haughty young socialite in a daringly low-cut black satin dress. The scene at the races in the film *My Fair Lady* was inspired by 'Black Ascot' in 1910, when the race meeting was held shortly after the death of Edward VII and the aristocracy attended in full mourning.

After Christian Dior's revolutionary New Look collection of 1947, grey became a big trend for women's suits in post-war fashion. The renowned Hollywood costume designer Edith Head, who worked on many of Alfred Hitchcock's films, said she always wanted to have the heroine/victim wearing a grey suit. And stylish women like the Duchess of Windsor and Marlene Dietrich embraced grey as a colour.

One of the most interesting things about grey in clothing, says Tony Glenville, is that the colour changes dramatically according to the fabric that's used. "Think of grey cashmere or silk and then flannel – school blazers. And then think of it in different lights. In the northern light, those Scandinavian shades work, but they look weird in the Mediterranean. Grey can go from charcoal to the palest silver grey. It's a more difficult colour than you think to get right."

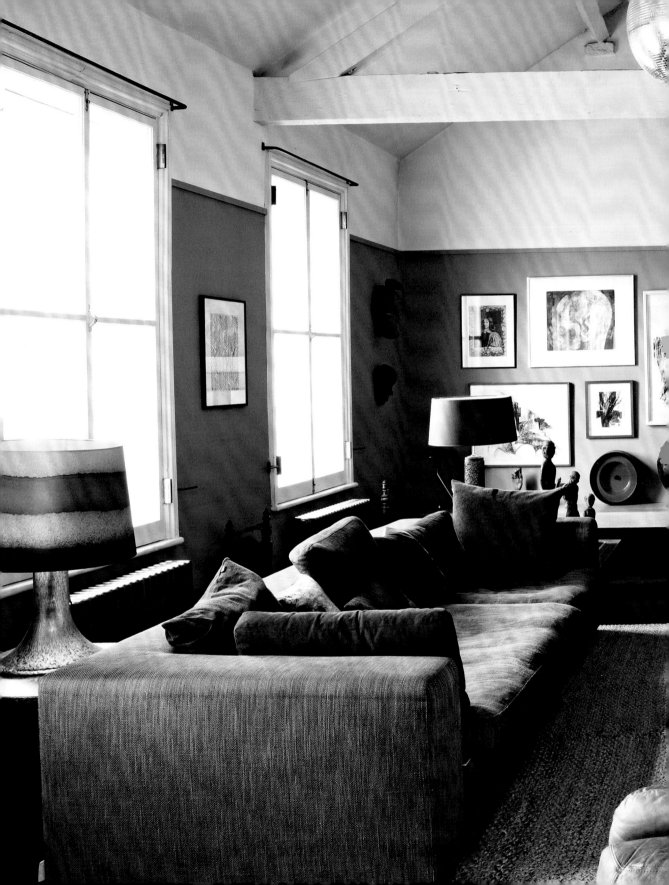

66 Grey paint is like the chocolate on a biscuit. Just as that will bring out the flavour of the biscuit, so grey brings out the depth of the other colours it sits with. 99

Marianne Shillingford, *creative director of Dulux*

Grey is the colour of half-mourning. In Victorian times, a complex and prescriptive etiquette of mourning evolved. Household manuals and ladies magazines gave detailed advice on the rules of mourning. In the immediate months after a close family member died, you were in 'deep mourning' and wore black from top to toe. After a specified period (depending on who you were mourning), black could be set aside and replaced with muted grey or lilac for the final months of 'half-mourning'.

It was the 18th-century English writer and lexicographer Samuel Johnson who championed the spelling of grey with an 'a', but by the early 20th century it had evolved into grey... in the UK, at least. Over the pond, however, the Americans still favour the 'a' spelling.

THIS PAGE AND OPPOSITE *Here the panelling is painted in Farrow & Ball Mouse's Back. Opposite is Elephant's Breath (also by Farrow & Ball) in the window recess, with Strong White butting up to it. Elephant's Breath is another colour that can vary wildly according to the light, ranging from the clear grey in this case to a more beige tone.*

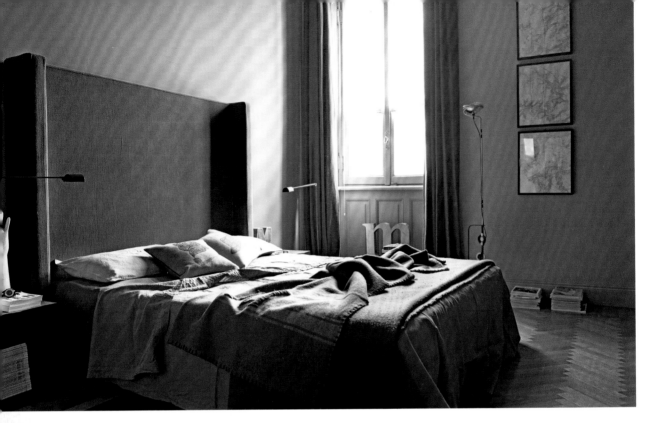

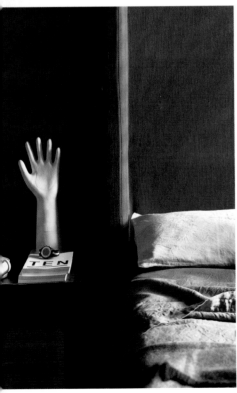

GREY IS
THE FUTURE

Let's return to the 21st century. Marianne Shillingford, the creative director of Dulux, says grey is now the colour of progress. It is, as she points out, the colour of building materials — stone, concrete and pavements/sidewalks.

Grey is the colour of our city environments and, as we have moved from a pastoral-based society to an increasingly urban one, grey is a colour that we are much more comfortable with. Hence the international paint company Dulux confidently offering 557 shades of grey in its paint range.

ABOVE *If you're nervous about making a bedroom too dark, then use a paler shade on the wall, such as Inox or Shallows by Little Greene, and have a dark headboard like this one that wraps around the bed to create a cocooning space.*

LEFT *A white piece of art, such as this hand, will be perfectly framed against the dark grey of the bed and you can build up the look with bedlinen in different shades. This also means you don't have to spend ages hunting out the matching set.*

THIS PAGE *Grey will darken in corners and alcoves. So a very pale shade will appear darker at certain times of day and in different parts of the room. Wood Ash by Little Greene is a warm pale shade. Cornforth White by Farrow & Ball is also light, but beware in a north-facing room as it can be cold.*

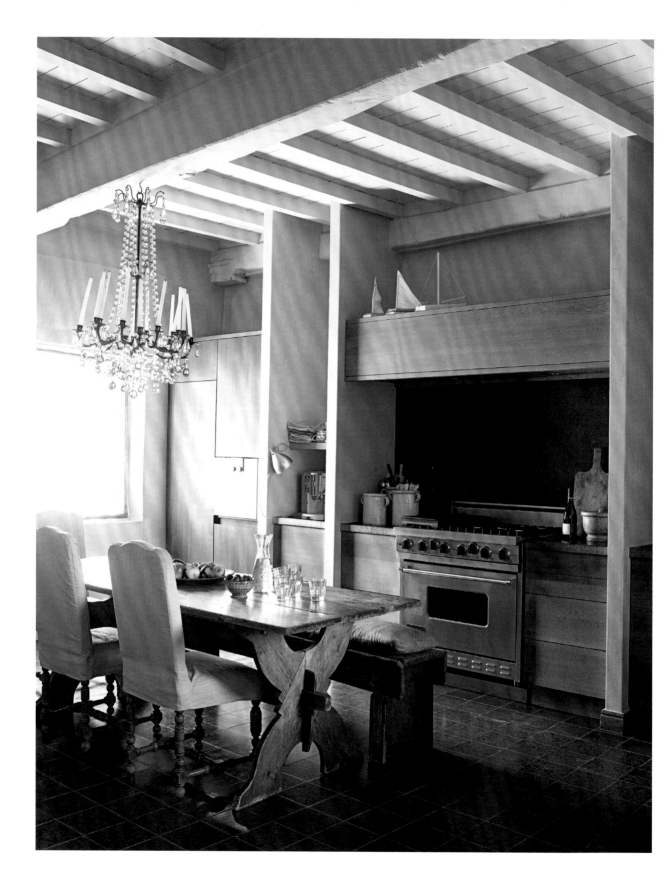

"Some of the colours already existed but were sold only in the Nordic countries where grey has been popular for a long time," Marianne explains. "Others are completely new." But such is the spectrum of grey that these new shades, which even have their own colour wheel, are actually called complex neutrals. It might seem that Dulux has done this just to confuse everyone further. Surely it's not even remotely helpful to have this much choice?

Little Greene Paint Company, meanwhile, is sticking with its palette of 28 greys, of which French Grey (warm and velvety) is the most popular. It is, says the MD David Mottershead, a carefully curated collection of shades and there's no need for any more.

Of course while it's the safe option, and perhaps the easy option in terms of colour, grey is also the one that requires a great deal of bravery. Some people just don't want dark grey walls. So for them, the hunt for the perfect shade goes on.

OPPOSITE *Grey reflects and absorbs the colours around it, so if you have chosen a black floor, you might prefer a paler wall. Polished Pebble by Dulux is strong enough to be grey but won't dominate.*

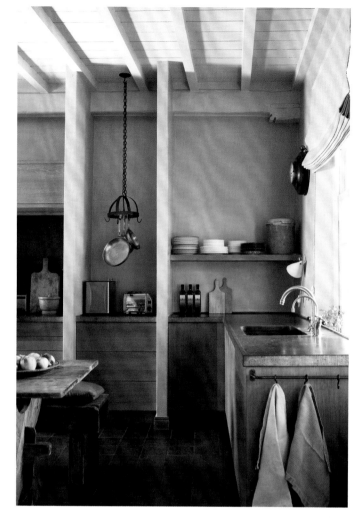

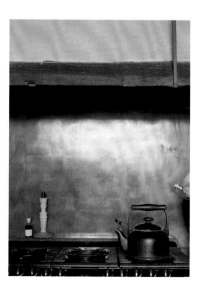

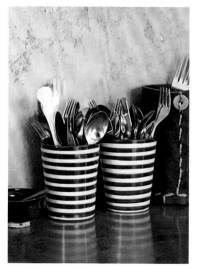

ABOVE *This room has so many angles that you need to either go very dark or very pale, otherwise it will be all shadows and the original colour will be lost. Another great neutral from Dulux is Rock Salt, which would work perfectly in a room like this.*

LEFT *Once you have decided the background colour, you can build up the look with accessories. Stick to strong monochrome colours for a co-ordinated feel and throw in the odd vintage piece to stop it looking too matchy-matchy.*

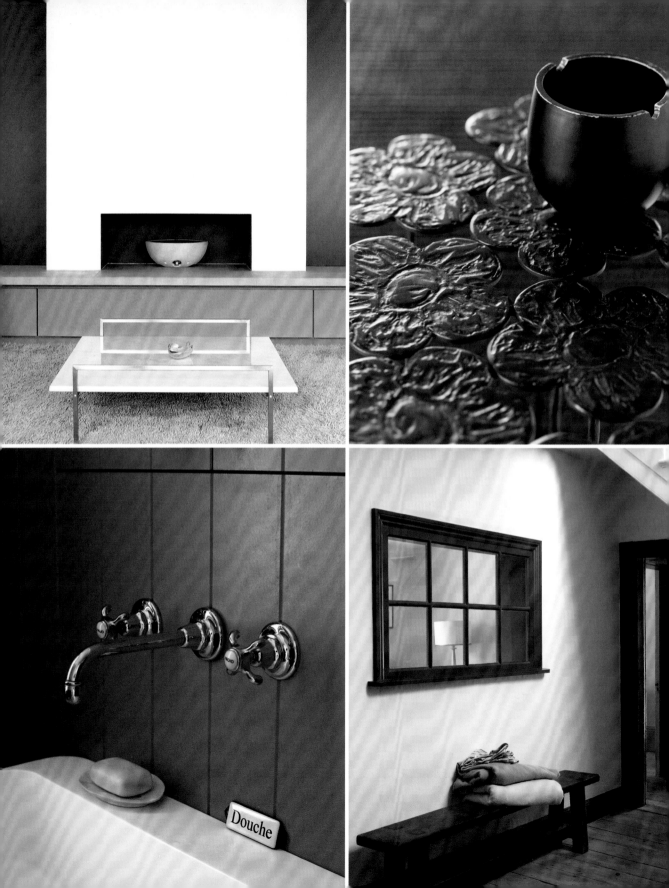

OPPOSITE, CLOCKWISE FROM TOP LEFT *Painting the wall rather than the chimney breast effectively inverts the traditional; Grey runs the spectrum from dark white to nearly black – somewhere in there is the right shade for you; Painting woodwork dark but keeping the walls white makes for a strong contemporary look; Even functional taps/faucets become a thing of beauty when framed by dark paint.*

RIGHT *Every colour goes with grey whether you choose rustic florals or simple geometrics.*

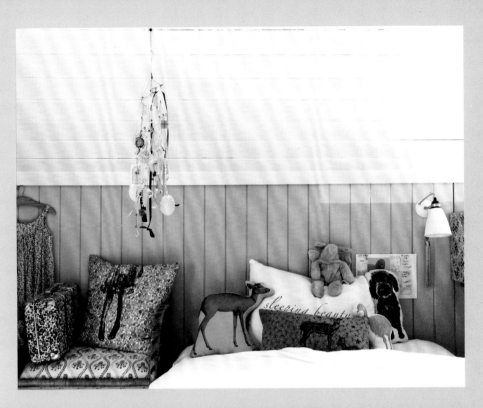

Expert opinion

Kimberly Duran is an American from Pennsylvania, living in Manchester, England. An interiors blogger at Swoonworthy.co.uk, she has used grey paint in several rooms in her house and is a big fan of the international paint manufacturer Dulux.

"My bedroom is Dulux Night Jewels 1," Kimberly says. "It's the darkest, chalkiest slate grey I could find, and I love how everything pops against it. Because it's not a true black, it doesn't look harsh but has an enveloping, cosy feel to it."

Sticking with the same paint chart, she used Night Jewels 3 in the dining room and describes it as: "A lovely sludgy grey with warm purple undertones.

If you are considering going dark but feel nervous about taking the plunge, it's a great shade to start with, as it works with so many other colours and neutrals. It has a similar effect to Down Pipe but at a lower price point."

Finally, in her living room Kimberly opted for Dulux Dusted Moss 2, the one she calls her "perfect" light grey. "It manages to lift a whole room that doesn't have a lot of sunlight, it's easy on the eye and works wonderfully with the original features. Another important point to note is that in a dark room white can just look dingy. A soft grey actually makes the room appear brighter."

66 If I see everything in grey, and in grey all
the colours which I experience and which
I would like to reproduce, then why should
I use any other colour? I've tried doing so,
for it was never my intention to paint only
with grey. But in the course of my work
I have eliminated one colour after another,
and what has remained is grey, grey, grey. 99

Alberto Giacometti

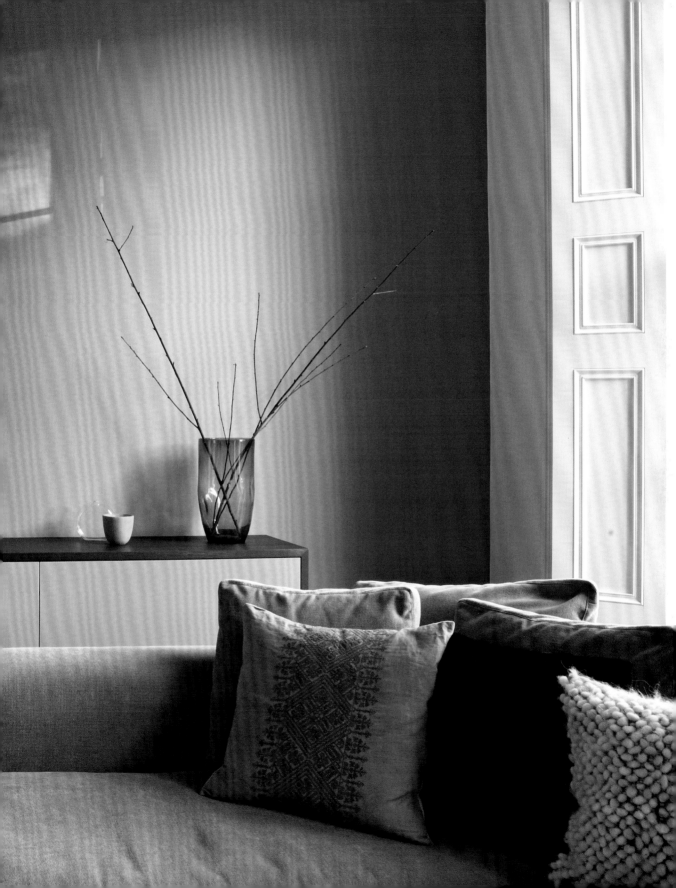

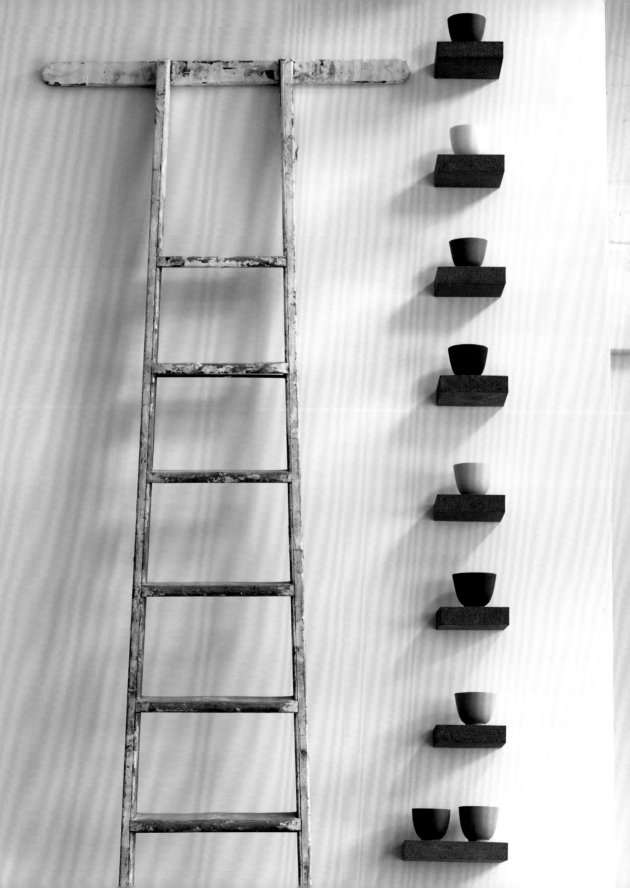

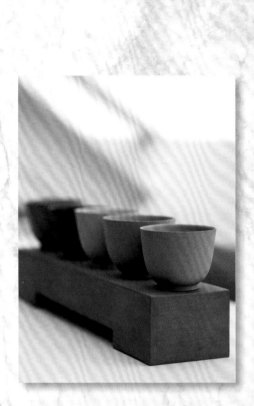

CHOOSING THE RIGHT SHADE OF GREY

Making the decision to go grey is the easy part. But which grey?
As colour expert Karen Haller points out, it's one of the most difficult
shades to get right because of the other colours that lie beneath.
Amy Wax, creator of the Color911 app, says: "Choosing grey has to take
into consideration warm light, cool light and the amount of sunlight.
What makes the grey palette so challenging is that there are so many
factors to keep in mind."

ORIENTATION: NORTH, SOUTH, EAST OR WEST?

The first question you need to ask yourself is how much natural light does your room get? And does that light come from the north, south, east or west? The orientation of your space will affect the way a colour looks on the walls and is the reason why exactly the same shade of grey paint can look completely different in different surroundings.

Take, for example, Elephant's Breath by Farrow & Ball. Some people rave about this warm, sophisticated mid-grey shade – indeed, I have a friend who has used it to great effect in her home. There it is quite definitely grey. But in my house Elephant's Breath is not grey. It's quite definitely beige. This is because grey is a complex neutral that changes from room to room depending on the natural light in a space. Unlike pale greys, which can appear cold, Elephant's Breath will never feel chilly or blue. But it might just look beige. Orientation is tricky... and it's the reason why sample pots were invented.

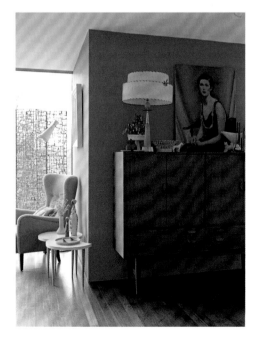

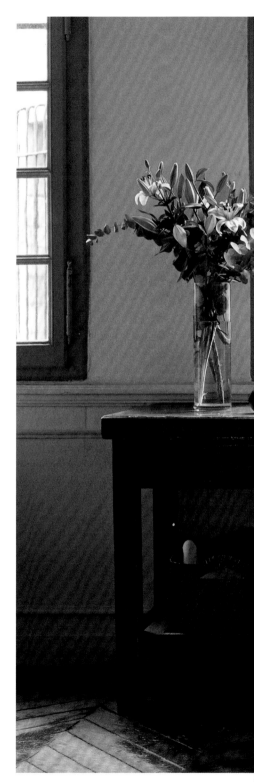

LEFT *Paler shades of grey will vary enormously according to the natural light in the room. If you have fallen for a cool grey paint sample for a north-facing room, you will need to find ways to warm it up with wooden floors and soft colours for it to bounce off.*

THIS PAGE *Just because window frames have traditionally been painted white doesn't mean they have to be. Experiment with a darker version of the paint you use on the walls, which will help frame the view outside.*

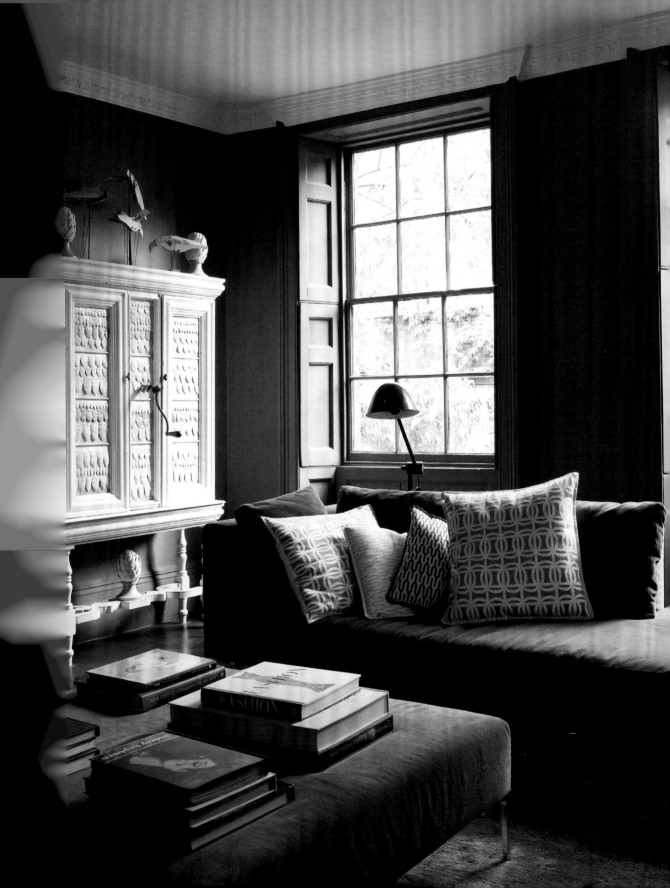

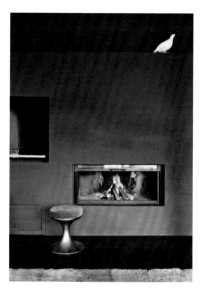

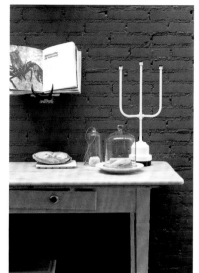

OPPOSITE *The owners of this room have stuck to a simple palette of grey, but by introducing pops of red, the room appears warm and inviting.*

FAR LEFT *The paint around the fireplace is Off Black by Farrow & Ball, which is softer than pure black and has no blue undertones.*

LEFT *Leaving bricks exposed and painting them dark grey is a fresh take on the classic industrial look.*

BELOW *Charcoal walls and flooring make a perfect backdrop for a marble table and sculptural white chair.*

NORTH

Light from the north is steady and constant (which is why artists and photographers love it), but it's also slightly blue. This is why choosing a pale grey for a north-facing room is tricky. Many shades will look cold or blue or nothing like the paint chart. If your space is north-facing, then steel your nerve, because when you find the right grey it will be amazing. But the chances are that you won't end up with the first one you put on the brush.

If a room is north-facing, small and dark, there's no point fighting the space. A small, dark room will always be a small, dark room, even if you paint it in a pale colour. Instead, why not embrace its cosiness? Pick a strong shade of grey – nearly black, if you dare – and put it on every wall. Do the skirting/base boards as well. You can keep the ceiling white and paint the floor white too, if you like. Now add a few mirrors to bounce the light around. And some metallic touches – brass lamps, or a glass coffee table. That will add reflection and interest.

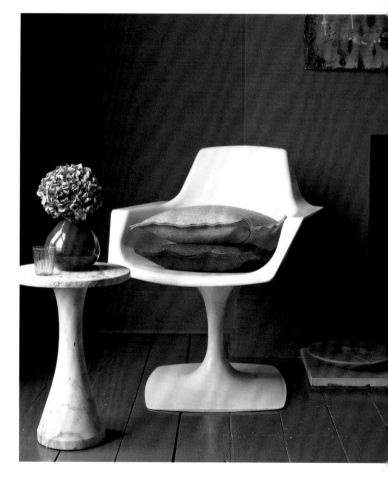

This quirky kitchen uses a huge range of textures including raw wood cupboards, concrete worktop, tiled floor and wall panelling, but it is all tied together with grey paint – try Storm Grey by Zoffany for a similar look – and the overall effect is rustic rather than modern.

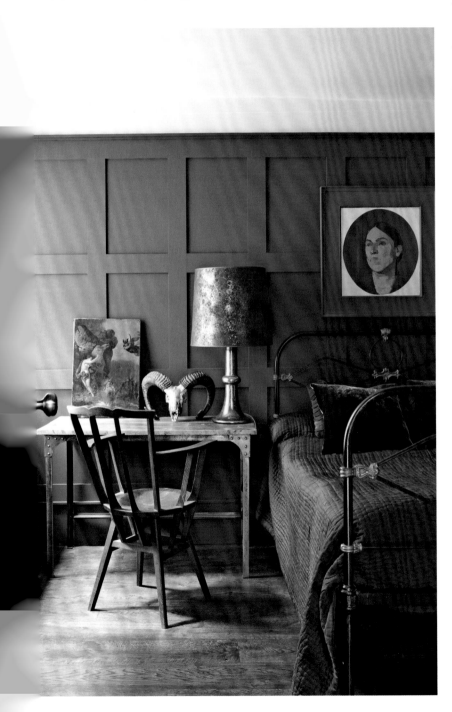

If you're feeling really brave, you could paint the walls in gloss paint. This will have a lacquer-like effect and reflect the light, making the space appear bigger. Another trick is to paint the ceiling in dark gloss paint. It used to be thought that this would make the ceiling look lower, but actually the opposite is true. And it creates another focal point. The ceiling is, after all, the fifth wall, and this effect can really highlight a great pendant light. If you want to try this, choose a grey with a hint of stone or beige, as those pigments will warm up when the electric light goes on and make the room feel inviting and cosy.

Marianne Shillingford, creative director at Dulux, has some wise words when it comes to working with grey. It's like cooking, she says: it's all about what you put with it. So, if you have a north-facing room and you want to paint it pale grey, which can end up looking cold, you need to be clever with the lighting. And if you add texture in the form of natural wood and warm fabrics, you will give the grey something to bounce off and it will warm it up.

LEFT *A simple panelled wall takes on a more dramatic appearance when painted in a dark grey such as Railings by Farrow & Ball. The brass lamp reflects light from the window at the side to stop the room being too dark.*

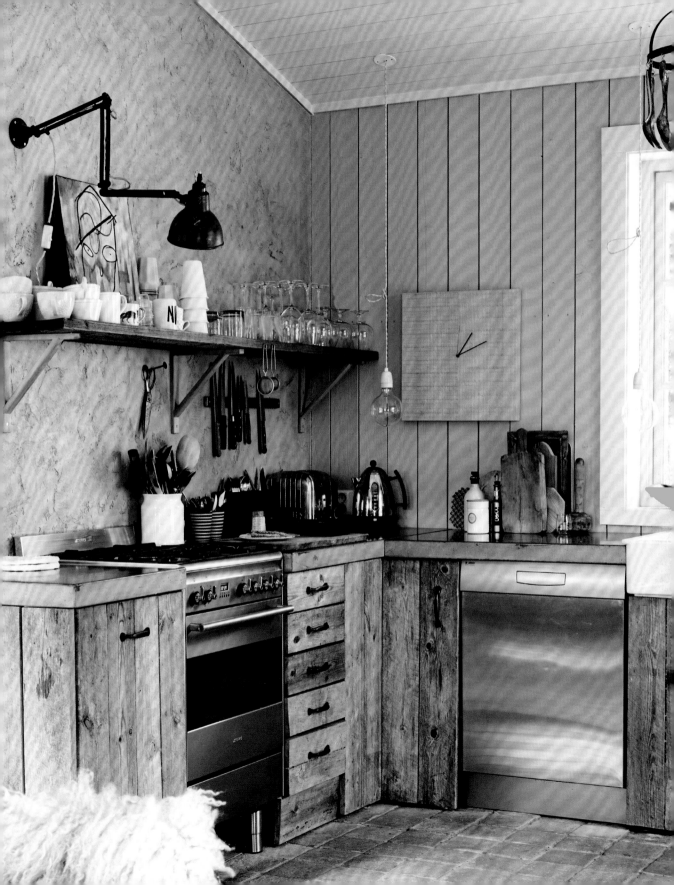

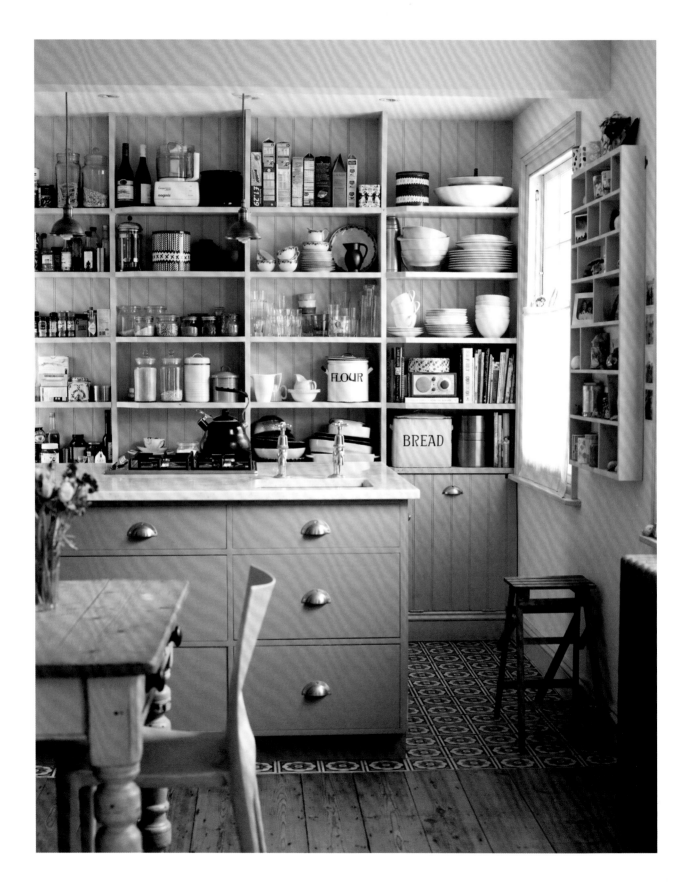

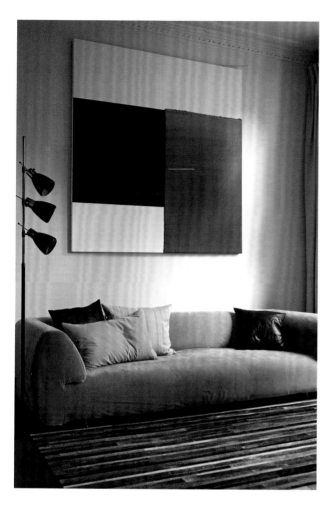

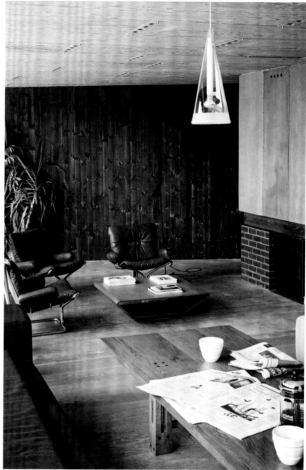

I can attest to this. During one of my grey kitchen phases, I painted the walls a very pale grey. The kitchen is north-facing and the result was cold, dull and made everyone feel a bit miserable. Our kitchen is used mostly in the day; when the lights are on, they are basic downlighting LEDs. There is nothing subtle about them. The worktops are stainless steel and there is, to add insult to injury, a tin ceiling. It's no wonder it was a disaster, says Marianne, helpfully.

If, however, I had added a few lamps at different heights – floor, wall and table, if the worktops were unfinished wood and the ceiling plasterboard, it would have looked completely different. Clearly those are changes that aren't always possible in a kitchen, but they are easy to carry out in a bedroom or living room.

OPPOSITE *Painting the cupboards and shelves, as well as the wall behind them, in the same uniform shade of grey means the objects on them really stand out, almost like a work of art. Putting everything behind doors would create a sleek, modern kitchen that is entirely different to this one.*

ABOVE LEFT *This may look like a casual arrangement of cushions on a sofa, but the graphic painting above emphasizes the geometric*

layout and shows how varying shades of grey work well together when combined in different textures. The yellow cushion could be swapped for any other colour to keep it looking fresh.

ABOVE RIGHT *Sometimes simple is best: grey is the only colour used here, but the textured wall, cork ceiling, floor rugs and leather chair all layer up to produce a well-considered space that doesn't need any more colour.*

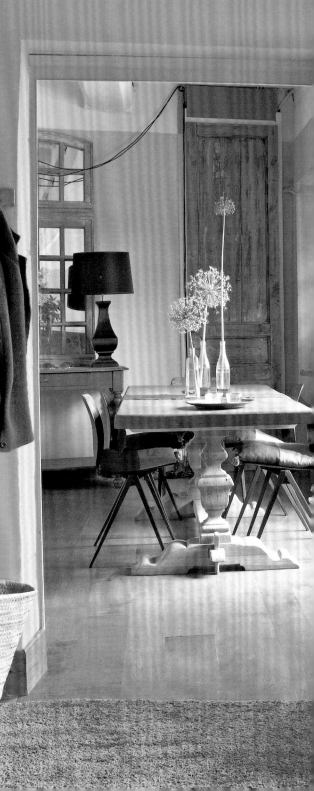

> **"Taste is simply confident decision-making."**
>
> Simon March, *founder of Colour Makes People Happy*

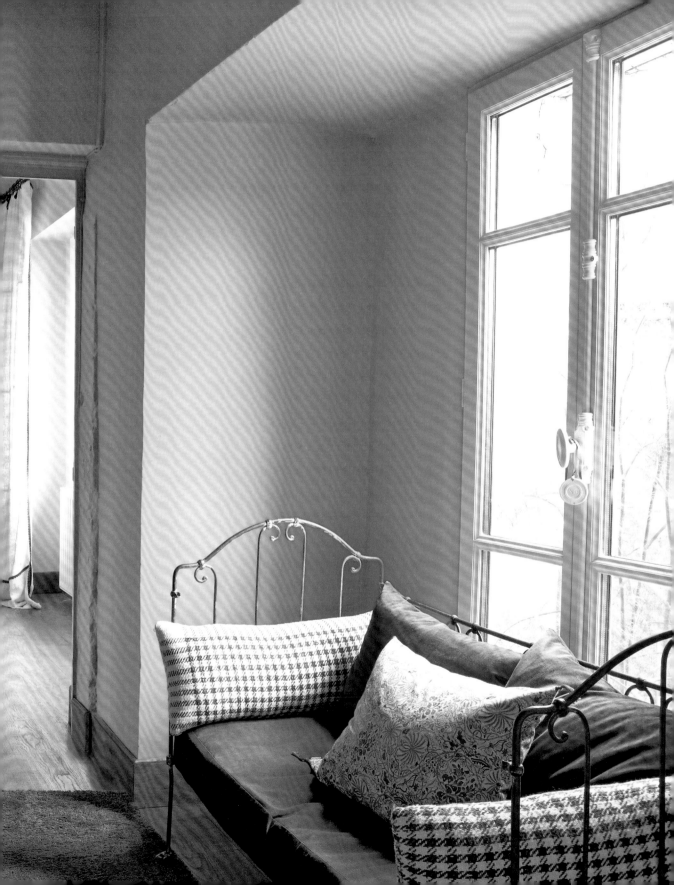

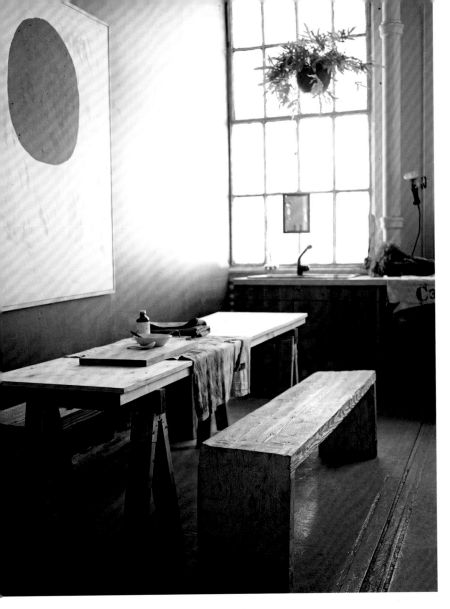

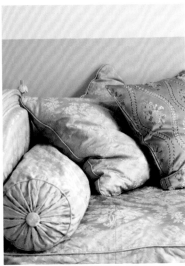

OPPOSITE AND ABOVE *You don't need to live in a Georgian house to have panelling. Rather than installing a fake version, why not use masking tape to create this rather more modern version in your own home? This is Hardwick White by Farrow & Ball on a background of Shaded White and it would be easy to paint over if you tired of the look.*

LEFT *Dark walls can be both cosy and dramatic. Here, the pale artwork on the wall reflects light from the large window and bounces it back round the room.*

SOUTH

It's not rocket science to work out that a south-facing room will be full of warm golden light all day, and this gives you much more freedom when it comes to choosing a colour scheme. Both warm and cool shades look good in a south-facing space, so those tricky pale greys that can turn a chilly blue or green in darker spaces will work well here and can be less dazzling (and less boring) than white.

Having said that, you can also go dark, because the amount of natural light means that you can have all the drama of dark walls and the space will never feel dingy. My own sitting room is a case in point – south-facing and painted a deep charcoal grey. Perfectly light and bright in the daytime, it takes on a wonderfully cosy feel under electric light in the evening.

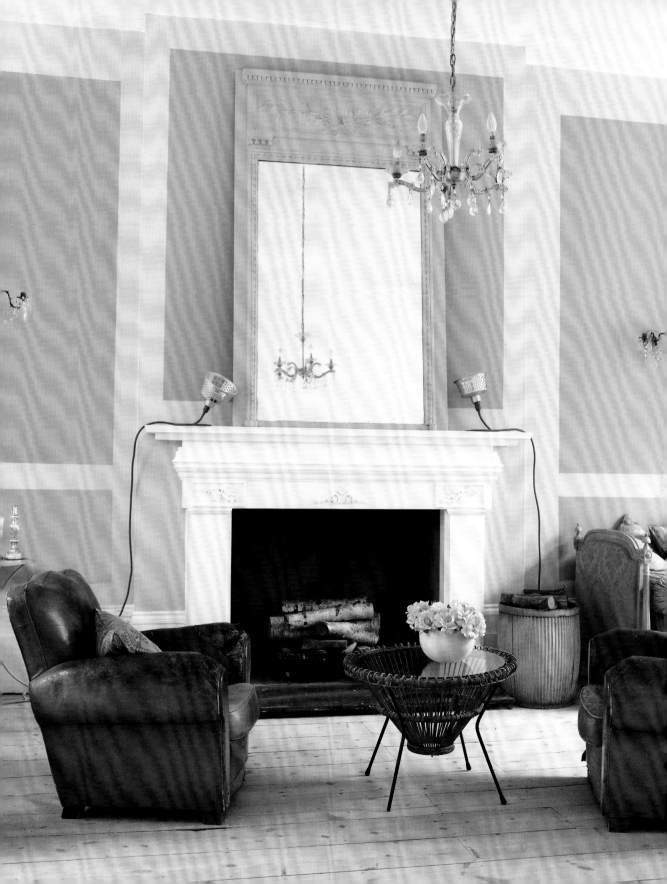

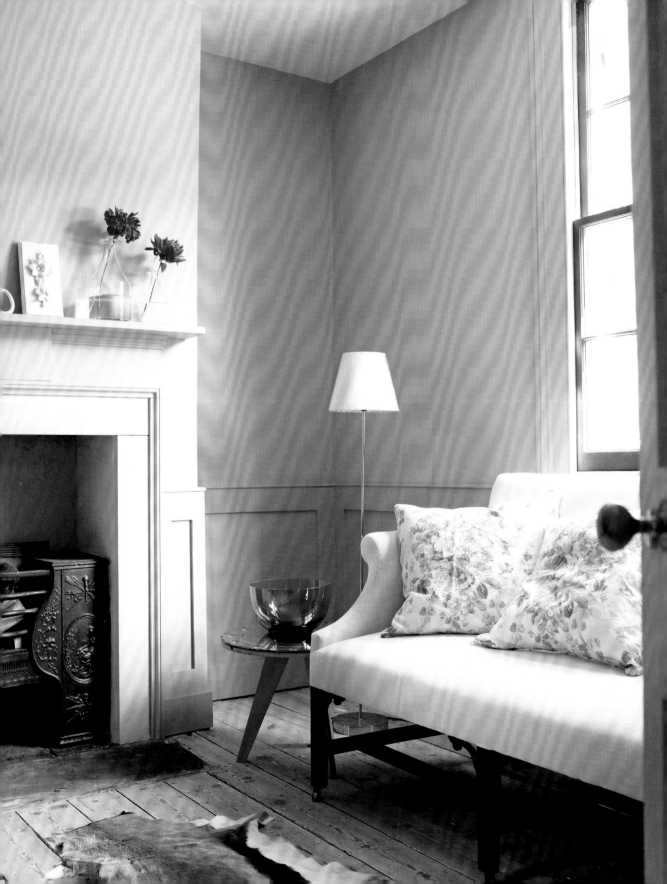

EAST & WEST

East- and west-facing rooms can be tricky, as the light will change from warm to cold or vice versa as the sun moves across the sky during the course of the day. If you're in a south-easterly facing room, the light will go from clear and blue in the morning to warm and golden in late afternoon, and it will be the same in a north-westerly facing space. Are you still with me?

Basically, this means that a warm grey might turn beige as the day progresses, while a cool grey could turn cold and hard. The secret is to find a shade that can warm the cool and tone down the warm. East-facing rooms sometimes have a blueish light, and if this is the case in your home, it's best to work with this rather than against it and choose greys with a blue or green base.

OPPOSITE *Here, the owners have elected to paint the part-panelled walls all the same colour, which is less of a cliché than painting the bottom half of the wall one colour and another above. This colour is very similar to Little Greene's Pearl.*

RIGHT *Little Greene's French Grey is a safe bet for a mid-grey that will never be cold and won't be too dark either. It looks clean and crisp when teamed with fresh white woodwork and works well in all types of setting, from rustic to industrial and more urban environments.*

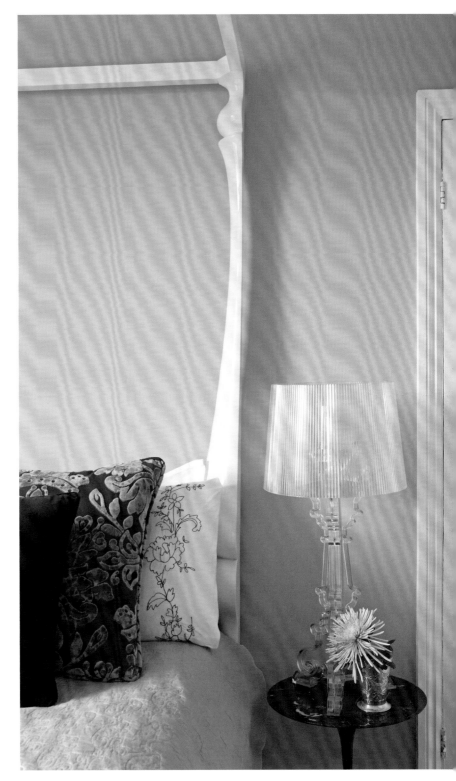

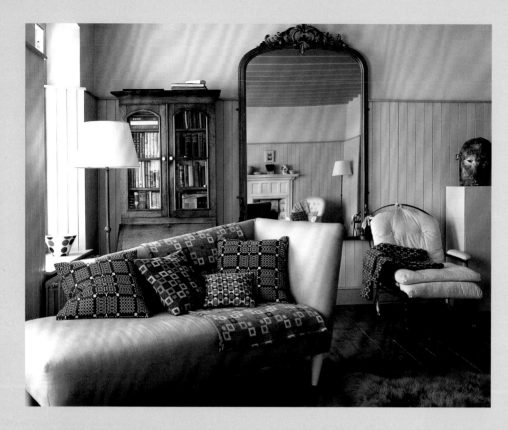

LEFT *If you're worried that a room will be too dark with grey walls, then a large mirror will help to reflect the available light.*

OPPOSITE, CLOCKWISE FROM TOP LEFT *Consider Dulux Paper Chain for a calm, neutral bedroom grey; Painting shelves dark will make works of art of everything you display. Warm Graphite by Dulux is a good match for this shade; This cupboard has been painted in Off Black by Farrow & Ball; Stone vases on a rustic wooden table are set off to perfection by the soft grey walls behind.*

∾ Expert opinion ∾

Hilary Robertson, Brooklyn-based stylist and author of *The Stuff of Life* and *Monochrome Home*, says she always looks for greys with a brown or pinky base, as the blue-based shades are too cold. *"The blue-greys can look a little institutional, but a green or brown base is warmer,"* she says.

A Brit who now lives in the US, Hilary had to learn to navigate the Benjamin Moore colour chart when she decorated her Brooklyn home, as many British paints were either unavailable or prohibitively expensive stateside. *"When I first moved to the US I tried to copy the colours I knew, but that never* *really works out well, so I learned the Benjamin Moore ones. I'm very keen on Sea Haze, which is a lovely greenish grey and goes with lots of things. It's a neutral with some personality."*

As for which shades of grey to use in which room, she prefers a dark bedroom and a lighter sitting room, but it's all a question of preference. *"Whatever shade of grey you use, make sure the skirting/base boards match,"* she says, adding that if you don't want the ceiling to match your walls, then you should do that in a paler shade of the wall colour rather than in white. This will make walls look taller and the ceiling higher.

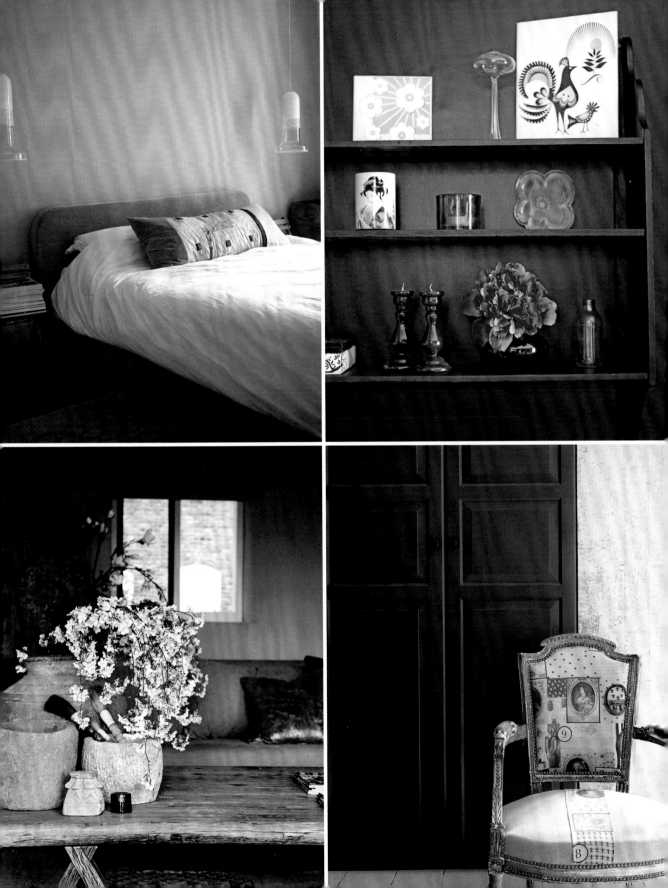

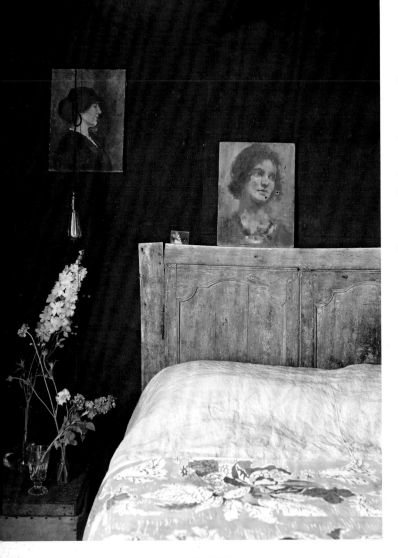

OTHER FACTORS TO CONSIDER

There is an oft-aired complaint about pale grey – that it isn't grey at all, but lilac. Well, remember that no grey is ever seen in isolation and consider the effect your existing furniture, textiles and flooring may have on any particular paint shade. In a room with a bright pink sofa, for example, the light will bounce off that and turn the walls slightly violet. Modern LEDs often throw out light with a blueish tinge and that will only add to the pink/purple effect.

If you are feeling brave, this gives you another option. You can deliberately pair a yellow-based grey with a purple sofa. Yellow and purple sit directly opposite each other on the colour wheel and so are complementary colours. This combination could look remarkably striking, although it might not be the most soothing. To stay on the safe side, stick with a warm grey wall and a red sofa to create a more harmonious scheme.

If you're not sure about orientation or the effect that your possessions will have on any given shade, the safest grey to go for is one so dark that it's almost black. This is because it will never look cold. Instead, darkest charcoal acts like a stage set, providing a backdrop for your possessions and showing them off to their greatest glory.

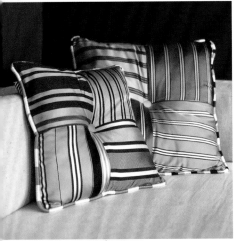

ABOVE *See how the pictures really stand out against the dark wall. It's an easy way to make everything look a bit more special, because these small pictures just wouldn't have the same impact against a white wall.*

LEFT *Even these stripy cushions look exciting with the dark paint behind them.*

THIS PAGE *You just can't go wrong with a pale grey wall and a raspberry pink velvet chair. The same colours can be seen in the next room, but with pink cushions on a grey sofa to vary the theme a little. This makes the flowers on the table really stand out.*

THIS PAGE *Grey loves other colours. Paired here with a rich burgundy, it is both dramatic and warm as a scheme. Keep the towels pale to offer light relief from the rich colours.*

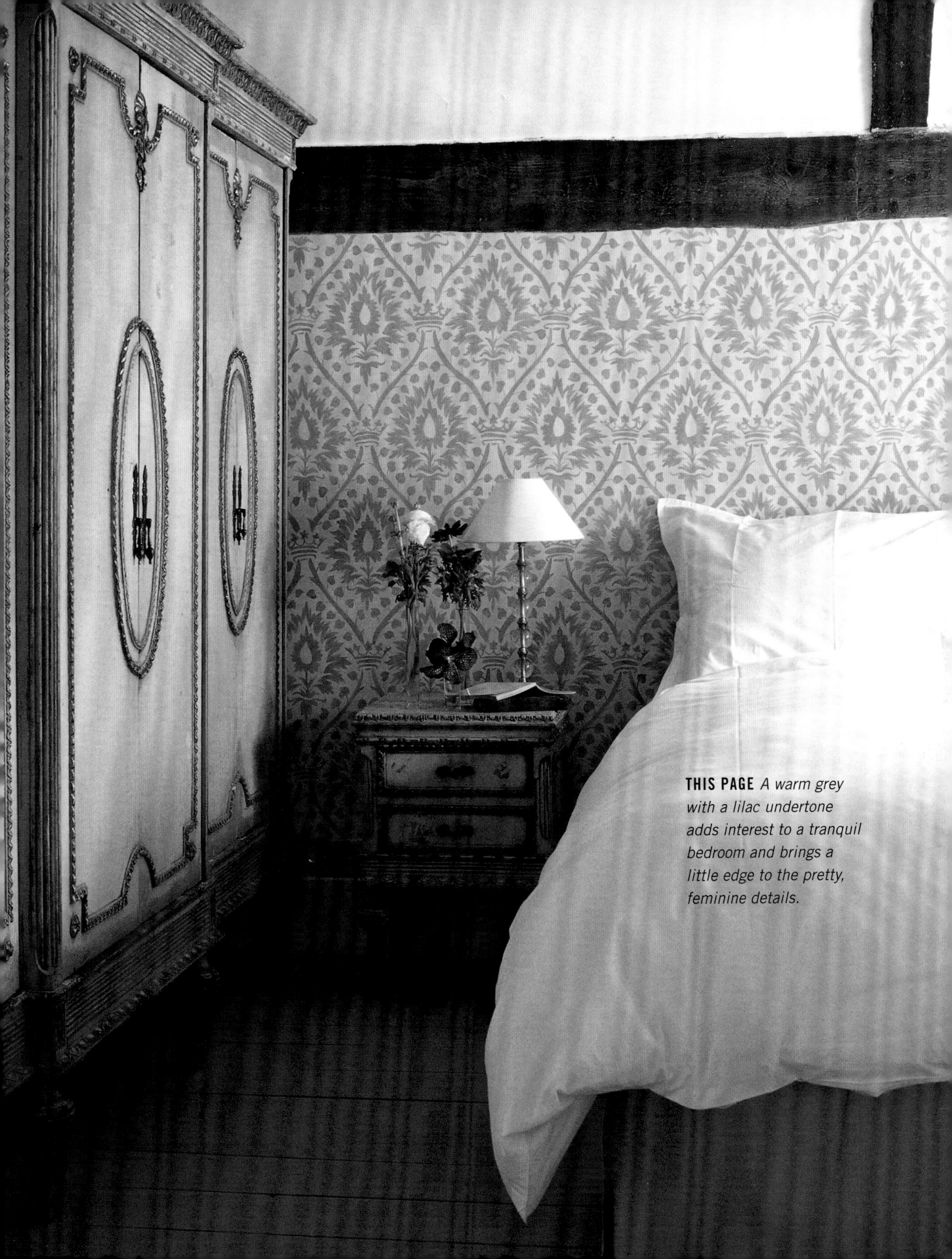

THIS PAGE *A warm grey with a lilac undertone adds interest to a tranquil bedroom and brings a little edge to the pretty, feminine details.*

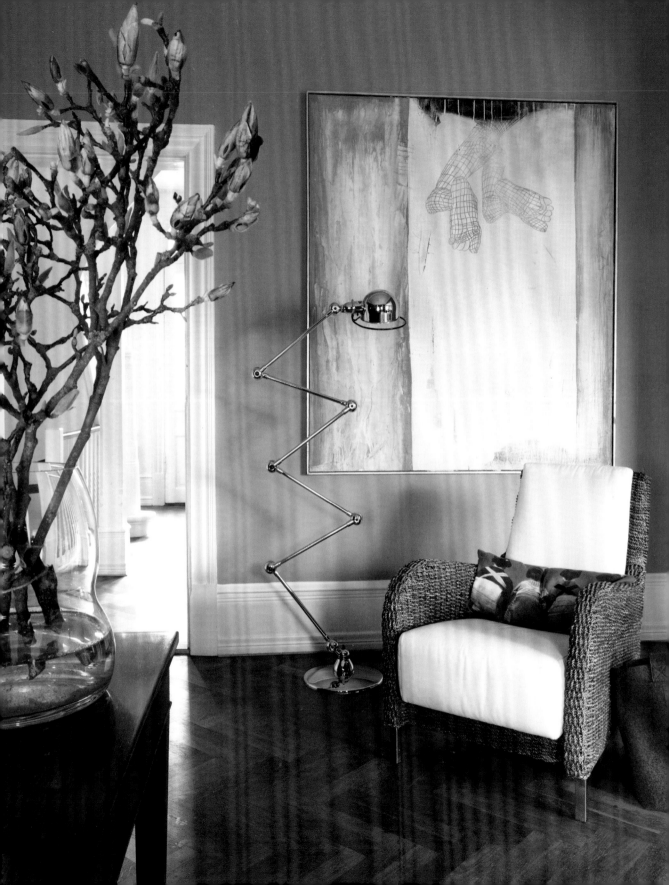

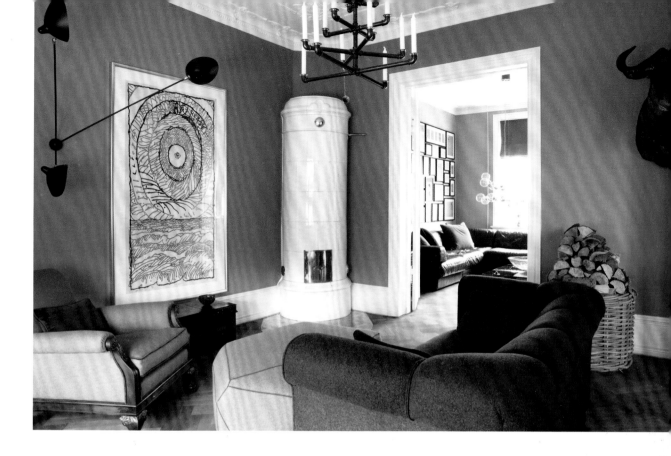

WHICH HEMISPHERE?

OPPOSITE *This room is painted in Manor House Grey by Farrow & Ball and is what the company refers to as a 'definite' grey, meaning it always looks grey in all lights. It's a strong colour that works well in homes with clean lines and strong architectural features.*

ABOVE *The room above is Plummet, also by Farrow & Ball. Here it has been contrasted with lots of white and the stark architectural lighting also works well against this shade.*

I appreciate that this might sound like a silly question. After all, we're only buying a tin of paint. However, it's no coincidence that the fashion for grey started in the northern hemisphere, where the cool light and the weather both work well with grey.

Soft colours and sludgy greys may work well in a northern climate, but in the harsh sunlight of Cape Town or Sydney, they can look dirty or dingy. The southern hemisphere can handle bright, hard colour in a way that never quite translates to a rain-soaked terrace in London, Brooklyn or Copenhagen. Basically, when the natural light is cooler, warm, soft greys with hints of pink and yellow work well. Closer to the equator, where the light is intense and clean, cooler greys with blue, green and violet undertones work better.

BELOW *Good matches for this cool, light grey are Warm Pewter by Dulux or Soho Loft by Benjamin Moore.*

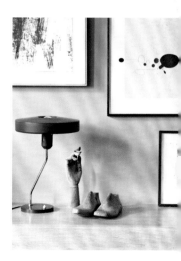

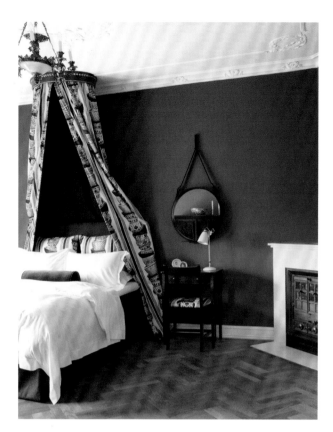

WHEN WILL THE ROOM BE USED?

This is perhaps the most important question of them all and one that, despite it sounding obvious, many people don't take into account. Do you use your space mainly during natural daylight hours, or artificially illuminated evening hours? You might think that it's no business of mine to ask what you're going to be doing in the various rooms of your house and you have a point. Up to a point. It's not so much what you are doing in there as when you are going to be doing it.

Let me explain. I tend to use my sitting room only in the evenings. My teenage children now prefer to hang out in their bedrooms or in the kitchen. As a result, the sitting room often lies empty from about 11am to 8pm. It is painted in dark charcoal grey – a colour that works brilliantly under electric light (which it mostly has) and behind a television. Dark grey also works well behind works of art, pictures or posters. It really helps them to stand out. If you have a room that is used mainly in the evenings, or where you nearly always have the light on, then dark grey is a no-brainer. The room is already dark, so you aren't actually making it darker.

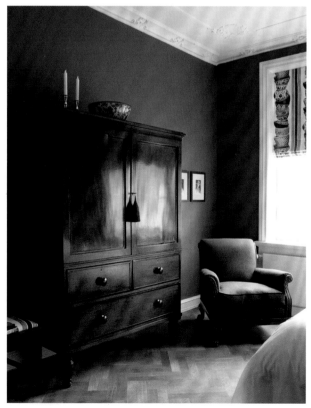

THIS PAGE AND OPPOSITE
Down Pipe by Farrow & Ball is the Madonna of grey paint. No need to mention the manufacturer – just say Down Pipe and everyone instantly knows who made it and to what colour you are referring. It's warm, it's dramatic and it works in modern or traditional, country or urban spaces. And it's good under electric light where it brings a cosiness to a space while making everything in the room look like it has been carefully curated. Try Night Jewels 1 by Dulux for another fantastic charcoal

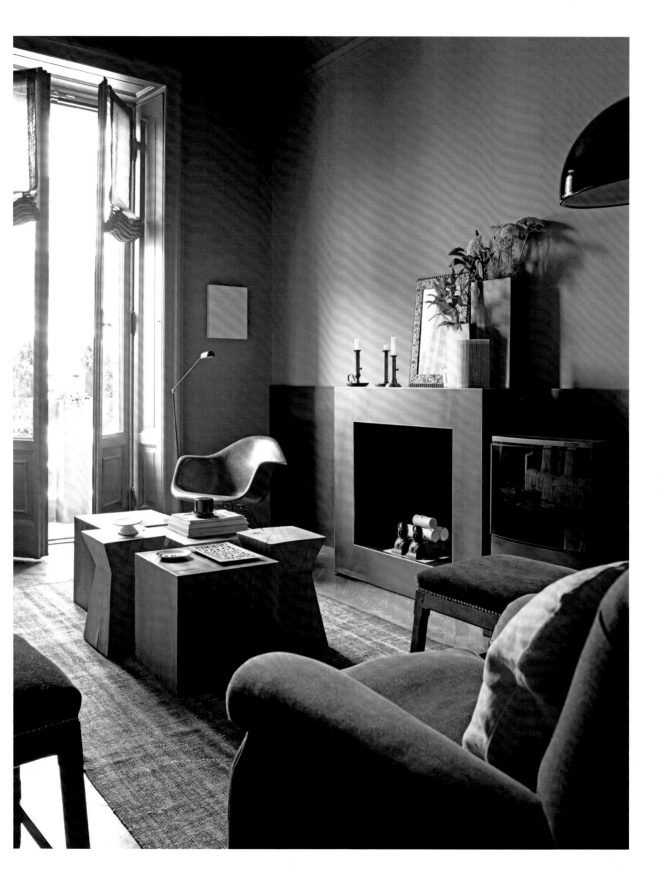

THIS PAGE *If you are nervous about colour but find black and white a little stark, decorating in shades of grey makes it much easier to introduce colour. I would never think of mint green, but paired with this soft grey it makes an interesting combination.*

Some rooms, of course, are in use all day long – the kitchen, for example. Perhaps you eat in there in the evening and then move to the sitting room. That means you need a grey that works with a combination of natural and electric light. Dark grey will work well, if you have a reasonably light room to start with, but you may not want to make a dark kitchen even darker.

There are two schools of thought on this. One is that if a room is already dark, you should embrace the fact. In a kitchen you can have dark walls and keep the floor and cabinets light. That will always look good. If a dark kitchen isn't your cup of tea, you'll need to go for a paler grey. This brings us back to the orientation of the room. As a basic rule of thumb, look for warm greys for north-facing rooms and cool greys for south-facing ones.

Dining rooms can go either way. They are often dark rooms anyway, and if you use them for dining – by which I mean evening meals – then you can go dark and intimate. If it's more of a breakfast room, then light grey is more of a breakfast colour. Bedrooms are also a matter of opinion. Do you want to cocoon at night in a dark, cosy space, or to wake up bathed in light, refreshed and raring to go? It's your choice.

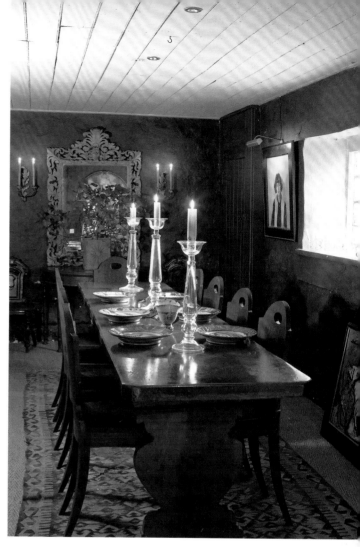

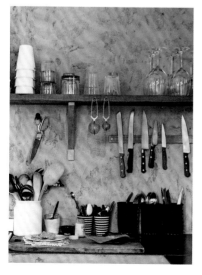

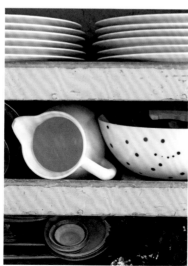

ABOVE *It has been said that red is the best colour for dining rooms, as it stimulates the appetite, but this is, in fact, orange. A dining room is actually the perfect room for a dark and dramatic colour – you don't spend that much time in it, so you can afford to be bold. Candles and crystal will bounce the light around.*

LEFT *If you favour the rustic look, consider using grey with vintage chopping boards and thrift store china. Everyone's version will be different, as they are one-off pieces.*

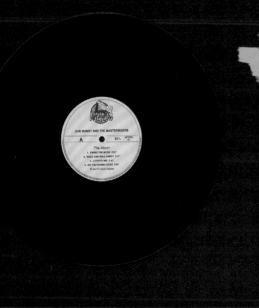

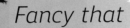

Fancy that

In the late 1930s, grey became a symbol of industrialization and war. It is the dominant colour of Picasso's famous painting about the Spanish Civil War, *Guernica*.

Grey is the colour of intelligence – grey matter – but also of old age and compromise. Perhaps all those things go together better than we think.

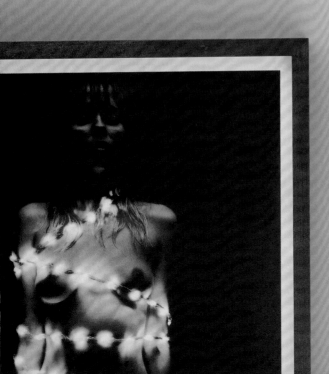

THIS PAGE AND OPPOSITE *Another example of how grey works really well with one other dominant colour – in this case red. While black and white and red is a classic combination, it's not one that is particularly relaxing. Swapping the white for a delicate shade of grey is easier to live with and more restful.*

THE DARK SIDE

Dark, medium or light? When it comes to grey, that's the question you have to ask yourself. And the simple answer is, how brave do you feel?

BELOW *I'm a huge fan of dark grey walls. They work in both daylight and electric light, and make even the shabbiest of sofas and simplest of chairs look more chic.*

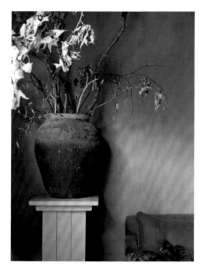

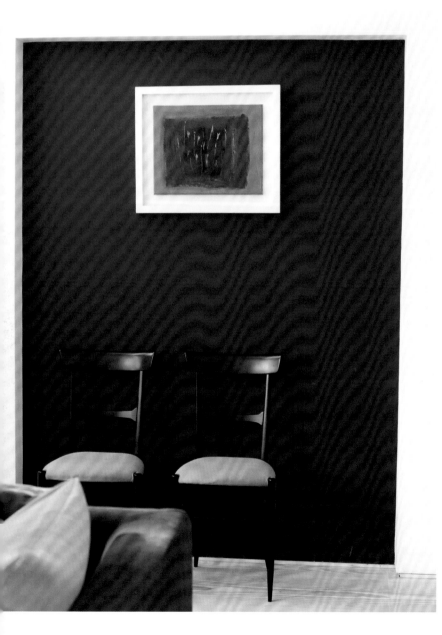

I tend towards the darker end of the grey spectrum because I feel very strongly that things have to look like they were intended. There is a danger that a mid-grey shade might look as if you chickened out at the last minute. There is also more chance that a pale grey will look cold, whereas a strong, dark shade not only shows that you had the courage of your convictions but also tends to be warmer. Darker shades can also, contrary to popular belief, make walls recede, so they won't necessarily make a room feel smaller.

Sometimes the compromise is to paint just one wall as a feature. This idea has been roundly dismissed by interior designers in recent years. They have sniffed disparagingly at the idea of just one wall either papered or painted and tried to persuade us to do all four. To which I say "pfft". If you want to paint one wall, then just do one. It's your house.

THIS PAGE AND OPPOSITE ABOVE RIGHT *The owners of this room have really embraced the dark side, but if this is a little too much for you, it's easy to lighten it up. Add some cushions and plants rather than dried flowers, and consider swapping the vases for metallic ones in either brass or pewter to bounce the light around.*

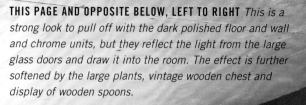

THIS PAGE AND OPPOSITE BELOW, LEFT TO RIGHT *This is a strong look to pull off with the dark polished floor and wall and chrome units, but they reflect the light from the large glass doors and draw it into the room. The effect is further softened by the large plants, vintage wooden chest and display of wooden spoons.*

RIGHT *Leaving the chimney breast white and painting the alcoves dark is a good way to make a feature of the shape of this room. Keeping all the walls in exposed brick unifies the space too.*

If you're only going to paint one wall in a room, I think it needs to be a grey from the darker end of the spectrum. It will bring visual interest and a hint of drama to the space, and make your furnishings and artworks stand out beautifully. Plus, I bet you'll end up painting the other three walls eventually, so it's just about easing yourself in gently. Paddling before swimming – that sort of thing. Starting with just one wall also gives you a chance to see how you really feel about a colour and to experience it in on a large scale in a variety of different lights, weathers and seasons.

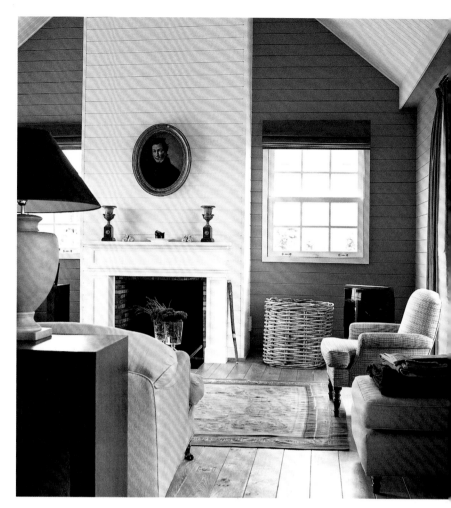

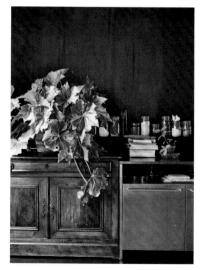

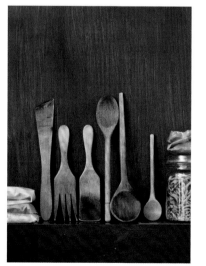

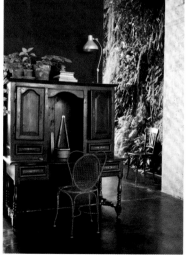

If you feel sure that you want to paint the whole room but are nervous about getting the colour right, then try it in a room that isn't used that often – perhaps a dining room, a study or the downstairs lavatory. That way you can get used to the colour gradually and see how you feel about it.

There is another school of thought that says you can afford to make a strong statement in an entrance hall, as it's a place that you only pass through, which makes it a good place to experiment. Also (unless you live in a mansion), entryways tend to be quite small, so it won't take ages to repaint yours if you decide that the colour wasn't right for you after all.

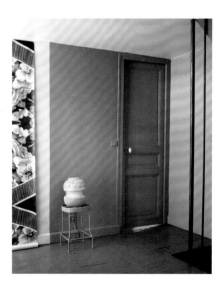

ABOVE *A door is primarily a functional thing, but by painting it and some of the wall around it in the same colour, the owner has created an interesting feature in this room.*

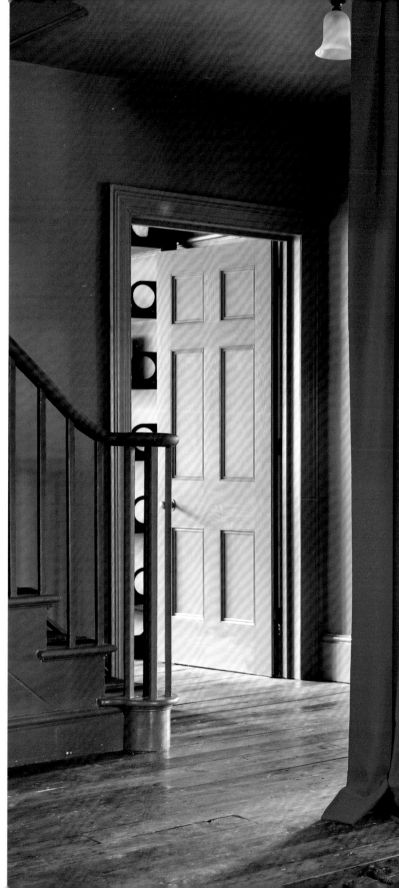

THIS PICTURE *This grey paint is likely to be by Emery et Cie, as this house was designed by Maria Speake of Retrouvius, the UK stockists of Emery et Cie paints. Try Urbane Grey by Little Greene for something similar.*

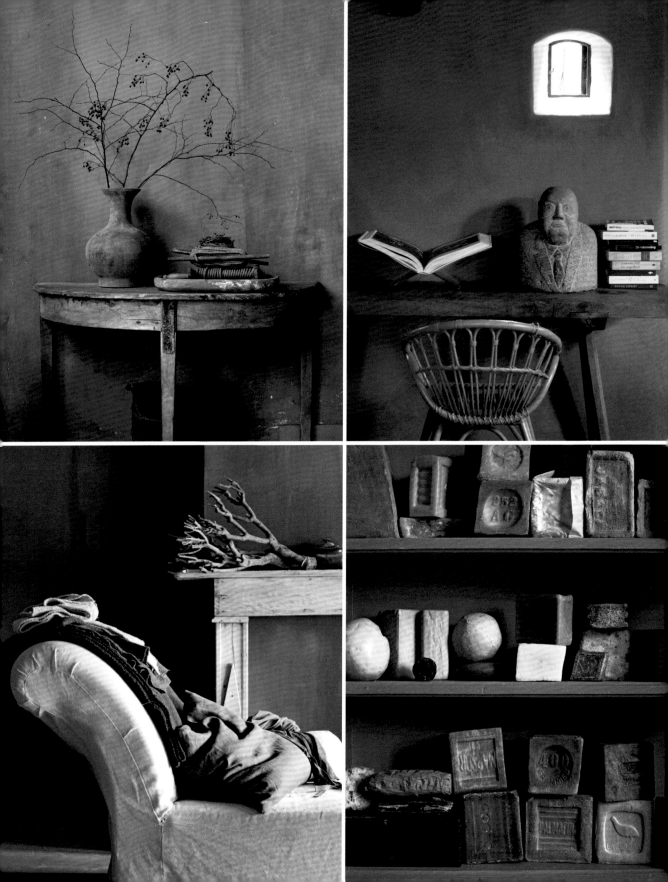

Abigail Ahern, the UK interior designer who is cited by Farrow & Ball as being a notable influence on the trend for grey paint, is so fond of it that she has created her own range.

"I started by painting just one alcove in Farrow & Ball's Down Pipe about eight years ago and that was it. I fell in love with grey really quickly – maybe too quickly, because we ended up painting the whole house from top to bottom in about three weeks. It was the best interiors move I ever made and I have never looked back. When you first suggest dark greys to people, there are often sharp intakes of breath and comments about how depressing or dingy it might be, but once they get past that and are brave enough to take the plunge, they often go darker and darker. My house is full-on black now!"

As for Abigail's perfect grey? Well, naturally it's from her own range, but then that's why she created it, so we'll let her have that. It's called Madison. *"It's a sludgy bottom-of-the-lake hue with undertones of green, which shifts throughout the day with the changing light. It's my all-time favourite colour in the collection and I have painted my whole ground floor and my Islington store in Madison."*

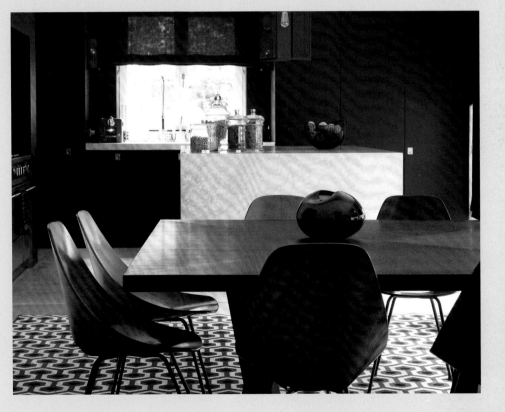

OPPOSITE, CLOCKWISE FROM TOP LEFT *This vignette in layers of grey looks like a still life painting; A rustic wooden table gives a more homely feel to this desk along with the grey-painted rattan chair; Dark grey will always look good with ivory – a combination that is much warmer and friendlier than simple black and white.*

RIGHT *A patterned floor is always good in a black and white kitchen. It's practical (you can't see the crumbs) and acts as the perfect foil to the dark grey wall.*

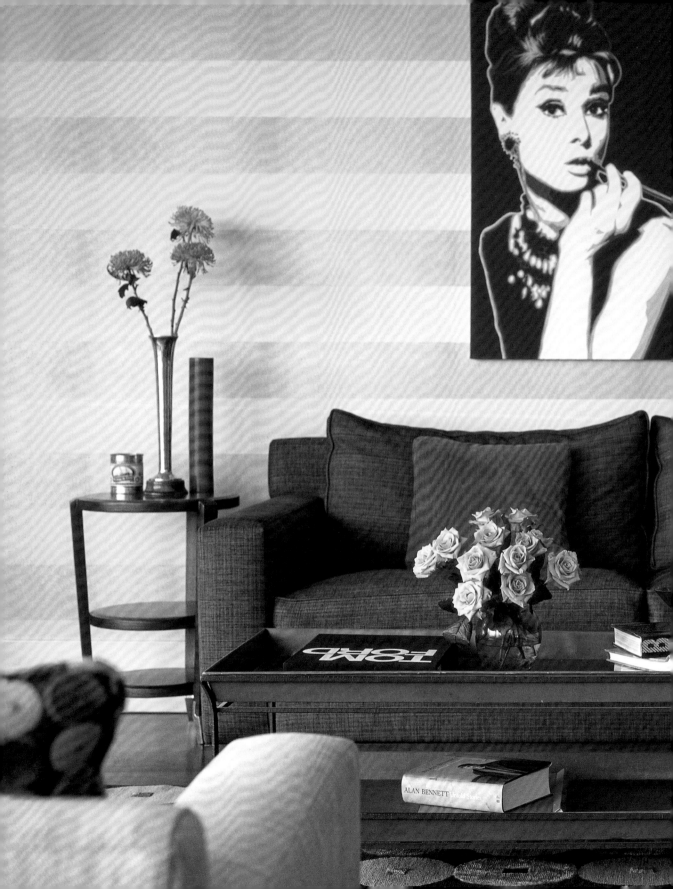

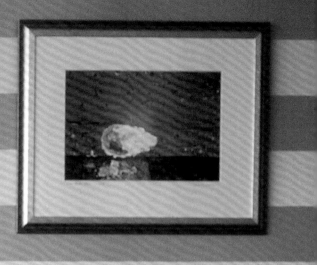

"Grey holds everything together; it is the perfect background – the carbohydrate in a meal. It is the pasta, the rice or the potato on a plate. But you must add the spice of another colour to complete it."

Laurence Llewelyn-Bowen, *interior designer and television presenter*

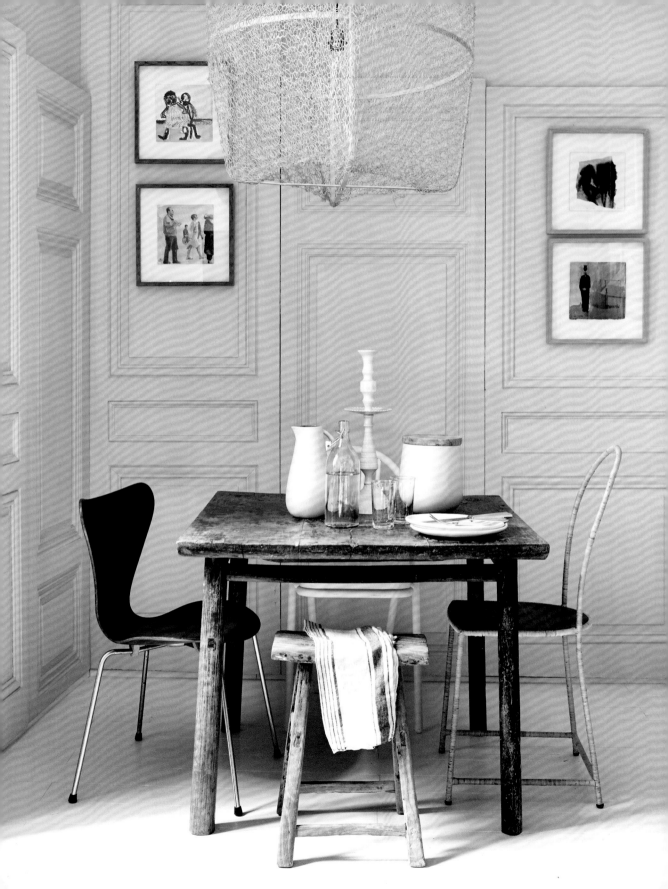

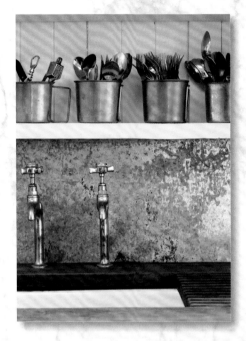

GREY MATTERS

So you know which point of the compass your room faces and have taken into account which hemisphere you live in and which sort of artificial lighting to use. Now all you need to do is choose the final type, brand, shade and finish of grey paint, buy it and slap it on your wall. But it's easy to get bogged down in the decision-making process. Sometimes you just need to suck it and see.

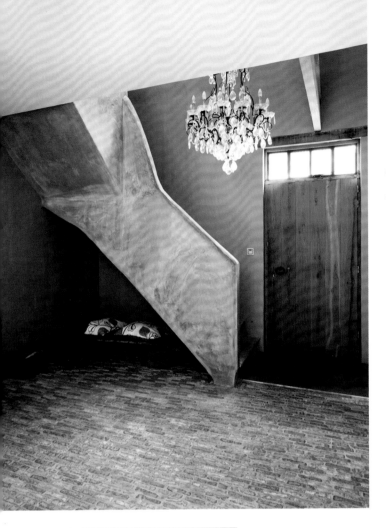

DON'T MAKE
IT MISSION
IMPOSSIBLE

A couple of years ago I wrote a blog post on choosing the right shade of grey paint. It has had half a million hits and more than 100 people have left questions asking for help.

These range from the impossibly brief: "Can you tell me which grey paint I should buy for the bedroom?" to the briefly baffling: "I live in Holland. I'm looking for an English shade of grey," and, of course, the bafflingly impossible: "All the carpets in my house are grey. We are now attempting to decorate the living room. My suite is light taupe and I have orangey wood furniture. Accessories are white with apricot and green. I have chosen a grey carpet, which doesn't appear to have any tinge of blue or green, to go with the suite, and would like a neutral, paleish, soft, warm grey that would look good with all the above-mentioned shades. I don't want a pinky grey because I may have that colour curtains. It has to be light because my husband insists on a colour that is a 'darkish white', The room faces south-east. I would be extremely grateful for some ideas."

In short, she was looking for a dark white neutral that is pale yet warm, goes with pink, orange, green and grey and will work in a south-easterly facing room where the light changes from blue in the morning to a golden shade in the afternoon. Reader, I have no idea what she chose. For all I know, she may still be looking.

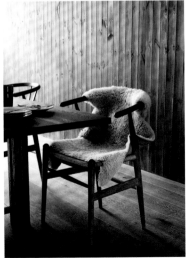

ABOVE AND LEFT
Painting the walls grey can feel a little intimidating, but bringing in lots of wood and textiles – such as a soft sheepskin rug – as well as adding an unexpected touch with an ornate antique chandelier makes it much easier to use. Darker shades of grey will always be warm and tend to work in both day and electric light.

THIS PAGE *While feature walls have been roundly dismissed by the experts (I say if you want one, have one) they still work in an open-plan space where you need to create zones. This one tones with the floor and the simple wood and grey accessories throughout.*

THIS PAGE *Now while I'm not suggesting that you prop a pile of paintbrushes up against the wall in a casual look-at-my-clever-display kind of way, this image does illustrate how a dark grey backdrop gives everything presence. Against a white wall they would just look as if you hadn't tidied up.*

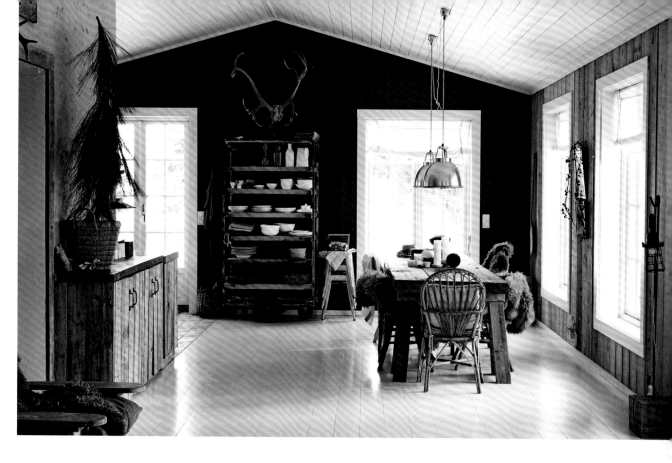

ABOVE *Painting the far wall in a dark shade makes this room look shorter and squarer as well as providing a fantastic frame for the furniture and windows. Adding lots of wood and metallic lampshades stops the room being too dark. For a similar shade, try Basalt by Little Greene or Farrow & Ball's Railings.*

RIGHT *Dark grey linen cushions sharpen up a shaggy throw.*

USING A SAMPLE POT

In an ideal world, we should try out possible paint colours by painting the whole wall. After all, it's that particular and precise combination of plaster and brick that you want to judge. Painting little squares of wood or paper just won't have the same effect.

Having said that, if you really aren't sure of which shades will work, then start off by painting large pieces of wallpaper lining paper (or cheap rolls of plain paper from Ikea) and stick them to the wall with masking tape, which won't leave a mark. Then you can move them to different walls at different times of the day to assess the effect or put varying shades together to see how they match.

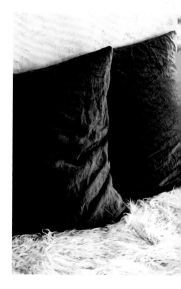

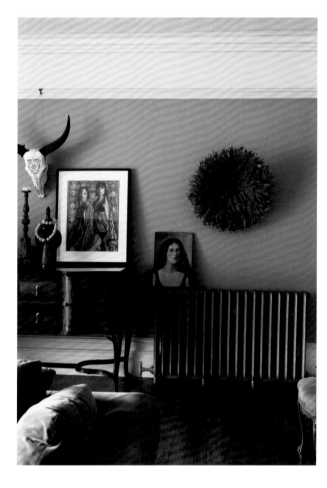

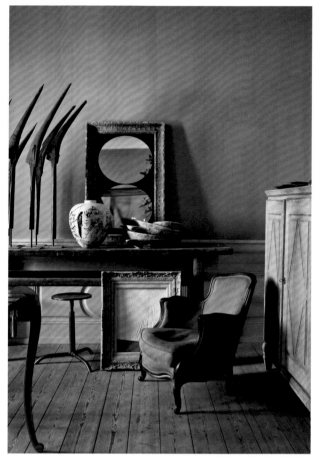

Once you've made a shortlist of two or three contenders, you can paint them directly onto the wall and see what you think. It's wise to paint the wall either side of a corner, as the colour will change dramatically there. Alternatively, if you're sampling really dark colours and know they'll be tricky to cover, paint the inside of a large cardboard box (or even a shoebox) so that you can see what happens to the shade when the paint bounces up against itself in a shadow and is intensified.

Hannah Yeo, the colour manager at high-end US paint company Benjamin Moore, says that once you've narrowed down your selection to a few final shades, you should put them next to each other: "This will allow you to notice the different undertones of each one, which should help you create combinations or colour flow."

THIS PAGE AND OPPOSITE
The point about painting with grey is that there are hundreds of different possibilities and each one will make your room look very different. That may sound obvious, but depending on the colour, your space could be welcoming, cool, urban rustic, classic or chic, just to throw out a few examples. Having said that, you can also change the look with your furniture and accessories. The red touches in the rooms above left and opposite serve to soften the room and provide focal points that keep the grey in the background. The picture above right is more architectural in tone. A single soft pink cushion or a green plant and a monochrome black and white rug would have totally changed the feel and given the grey some other colours to contrast with, which would, in turn, have warmed it up.

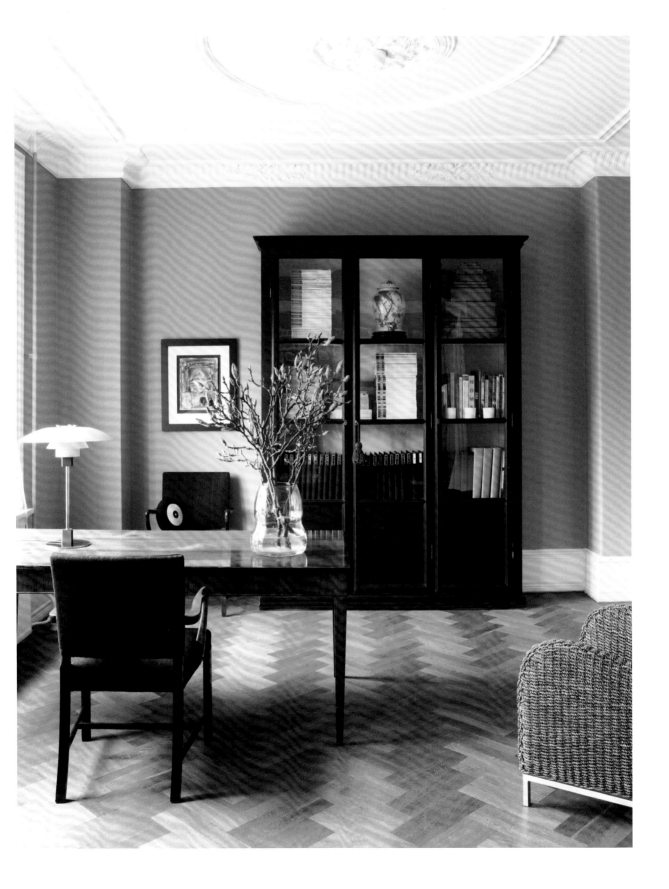

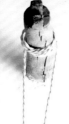

THIS PAGE AND OPPOSITE *The wooden panelling in both these rooms, one classically wide and the other narrow, helps soften the effect of the grey paint, which could have been cold in such a pale shade. By painting the wood, the room appears warmer and more rustic. Changing the bedlinen for different colours would soften it further, while adding layers of grey bedding would create an elegant sculptural feel.*

Fancy that

'Grisaille' is the term for a painting executed entirely in shades of grey. During the Renaissance, the technique was often employed in large decorative schemes to imitate classical relief sculpture, as even an expensive painter was cheaper than carving stone.

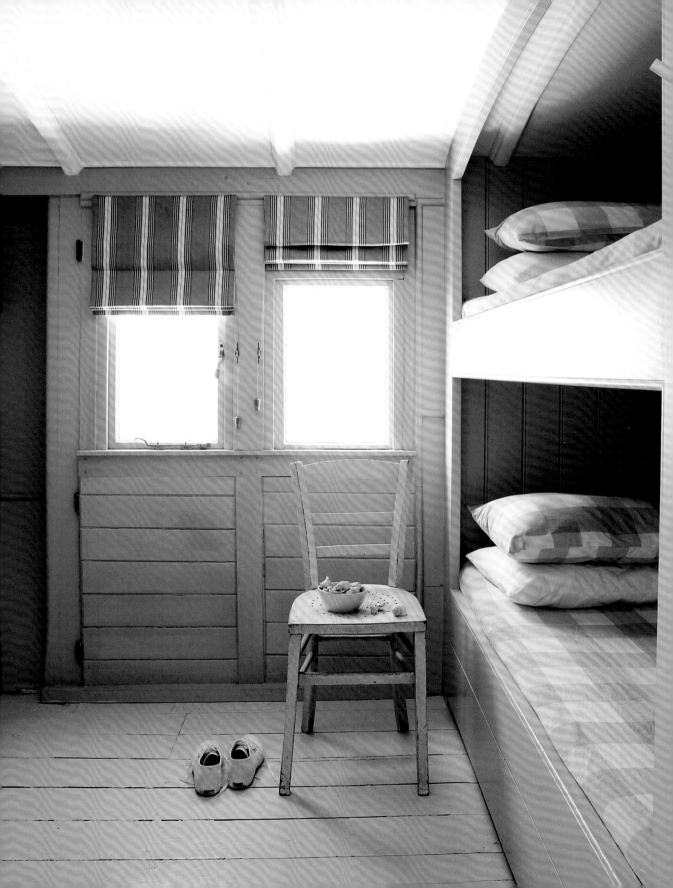

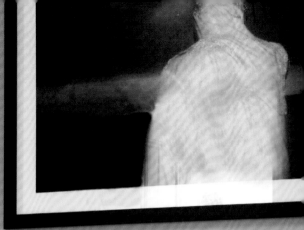

THIS PAGE *This is a very good example of how grey gets darker when it bounces off other colours. Here the walls are Hardwick White by Farrow & Ball, while the floor is Cornforth White and the woodwork is Pointing. Hardwick White is, according to the manufacturers, definitely a traditional grey, but it often looks beige until you see it in situ.*

CHOOSING
A FINISH

When you buy paint, you're not just picking a colour but choosing a finish too. Matt or flat emulsion paint is the most fashionable look at the moment, and the flatter the finish the better. It is the least reflective interior paint and has a subtle, velvety texture. In its favour, it will conceal bumpy or uneven walls much better than the others. However, it will also be harder to clean any dirty marks off. If you have chosen a very pale shade, you might want to invest heavily in baby wipes.

Thanks to its durability, gloss or semi-gloss paint is traditionally used on windows, doors, mouldings and trims. However, it can also have great impact when used on walls. It will reflect any available light from the window around the space and can also look like lacquer, i.e. expensive and luxurious.

An eggshell or soft sheen finish is more practical than matt paint, as it will wipe clean. This makes it ideal for busier areas that see a lot of use, such as hallways and family rooms, but there is also a danger that grey eggshell can give rather an institutional look – think schools, hospitals and, er, police stations.

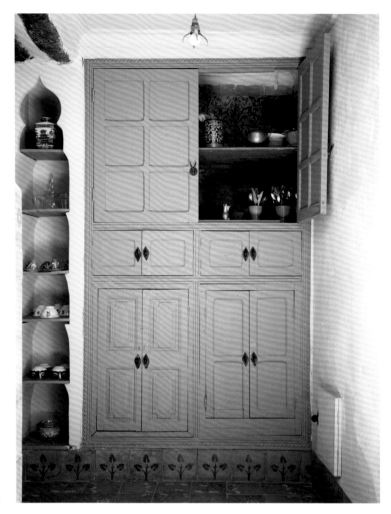

ABOVE *The kitchen in designer Agnes Emery's house in Marrakech. Sadly we can't all have original architectural details like this in our homes, but painting the cupboard grey – Hardwick White would also work here – makes a focal point of a lovely old original feature.*

RIGHT *Half-painted walls are currently fashionable again as well as practical.*

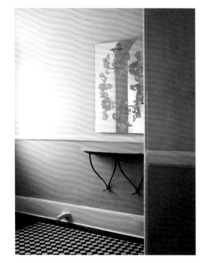

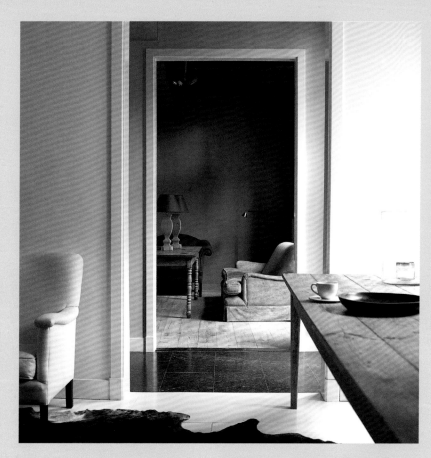

THIS PAGE AND OPPOSITE, CLOCKWISE FROM LEFT *These rooms demonstrate that grey doesn't have to be the colour of rainy cities and architects' homes. This is a classic technique for houses where the rooms flow into each other – painting one pale grey, then mid-grey and finishing with dark at the end; The reclaimed floorboards, shabby chic cupboard and muslin drape soften the dark grey paint in this bathroom; These two black decorative trees are the perfect accent for this stone mantelpiece. Every room should have a touch of black; Painting the alcove in this bedroom a darker shade of grey makes a feature of it and it's a nice change not to see shelves in the alcove but to use it to frame the chest of drawers and mirror; This dark grey room is softened by the pink picture on the wall and the plant. The statue provides an analogue touch next to the high-tech computer screen.*

Expert opinion

Daniel Hopwood, architectural designer, presenter of *The Great Interior Design Challenge* and president of the BIID (British Institute of Interior Design), recalls an early foray into grey paint. *"I was barely a teenager – yes, I started early. I decided to experiment because I felt that cream and mushroom was the choice of my elders and was not cool. At the time I was also dabbling with primaries and wanted a neutral that would offset these colours, so in my precocious world I decided to have an adventure with grey.*

Sadly, the result was a bit of a disaster; my room felt drab and institutionalized, although I wouldn't admit it. However, I did learn that in overcast Britain, selecting the right grey needs some thought.

Keen to avoid those moody teenage years, these days I tend to go for warmer greys, but nothing too overheated so that they don't clash with the bold colours for which grey is such a good supporting act. I also prefer to go for darker greys, as the lighter version feels lukewarm and not sure what it's meant to be doing."

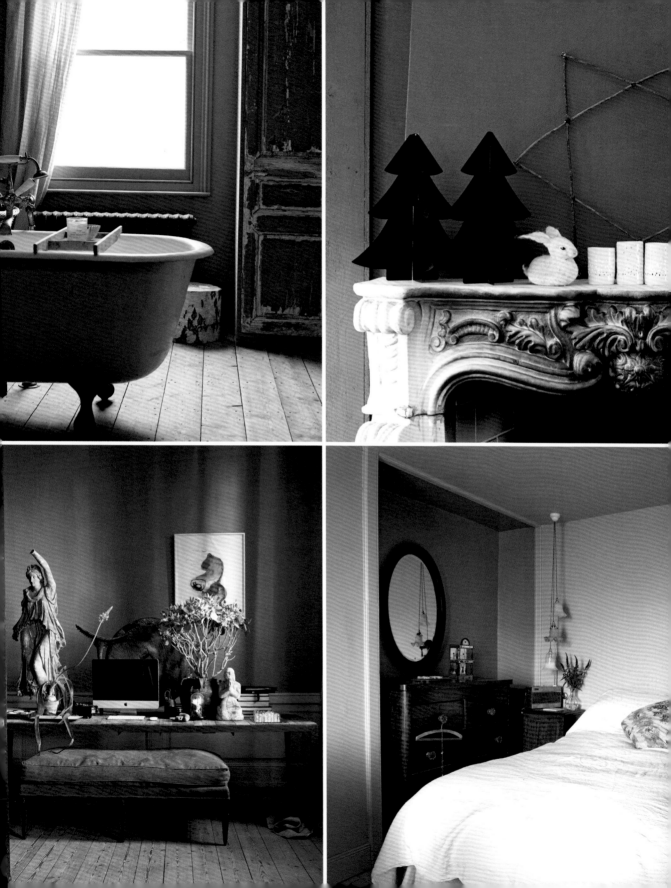

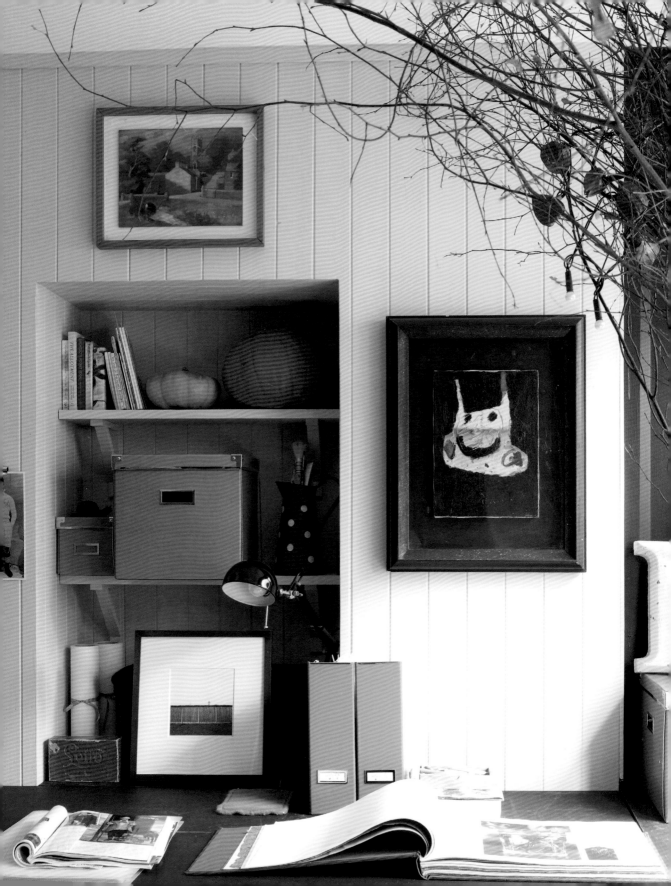

WHAT GOES WITH GREY?

So what goes with grey? Well, that's an easy one. Everything. As long as your base notes don't jar, you can pair grey up with almost anything, from neons to pastels and brights.

Pale grey walls work with a variety of different treatments. Some paint companies suggest teaming them with white woodwork for a fresh, crisp look. Or use the same paint colour on the woodwork; this is known as the gallery effect and makes spaces look larger. Do the ceilings as well to increase the sense of height. When it comes to accent colours, bold shades look really dramatic against a soft grey, while muted pastels will make for a restful space.

Charcoal grey looks good with everything from neon orange to soft blush pink and even bitter chocolate. You can throw in some metallics – copper, brass or pewter all have a particular affinity for darker greys – and vibrant patterns, or keep it very monochrome by layering up shades of white, black and grey for a restful, understated Nordic feel. "Grey is the perfect springboard," says Laurence Llewelyn-Bowen, whose bestselling paint is a slate grey called Clooney (yes, after George). "You can add flamingo pink or yellow, pistachio or lavender. It will last for ever – just change the shades around it and the accessories as often as you like."

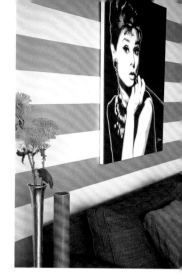

ABOVE *If you're feeling really brave and willing to make a statement, try some horizontal stripes on your wall. It will work wonders for a long narrow room.*

OPPOSITE AND RIGHT
Grey is the most versatile of colours. You can do as the Danes do and layer up shades of grey with black and white and then just a few accents of soft colour. This is the architectural approach. Or you can pick your grey for the walls and then hurl a bunch of other colours into the room and it will frame them all beautifully. Whether you choose to keep the colours geometric and simple or add a riot of flowers, grey will welcome them all with open arms.

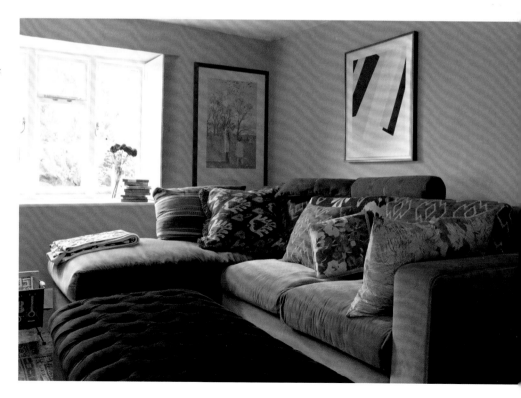

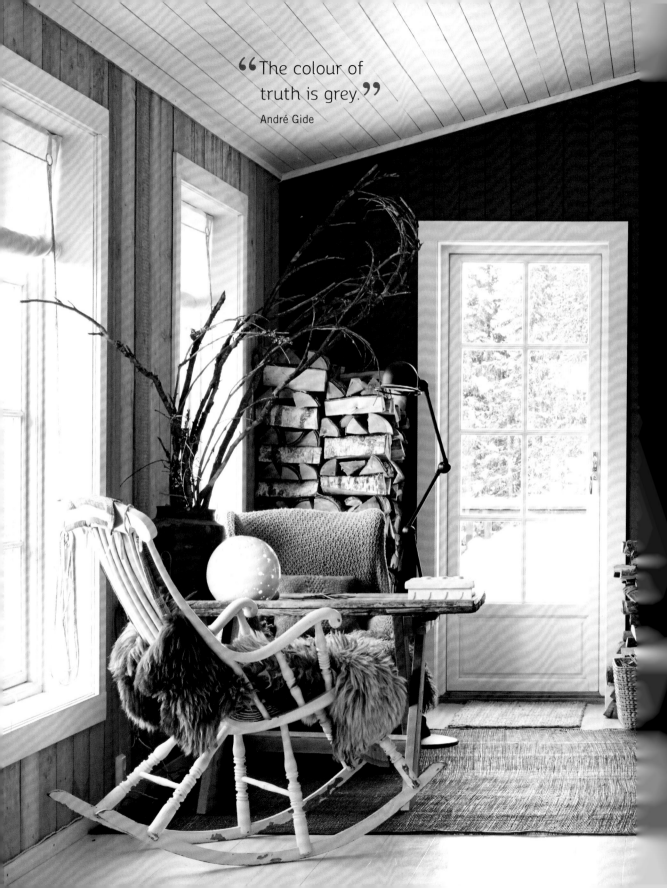

> "The colour of
> truth is grey."
>
> André Gide

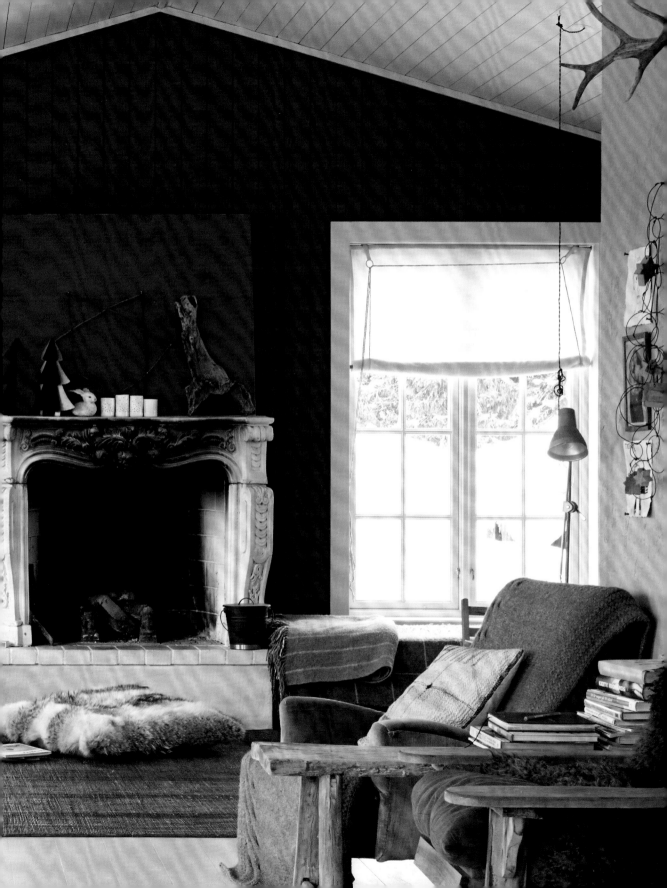

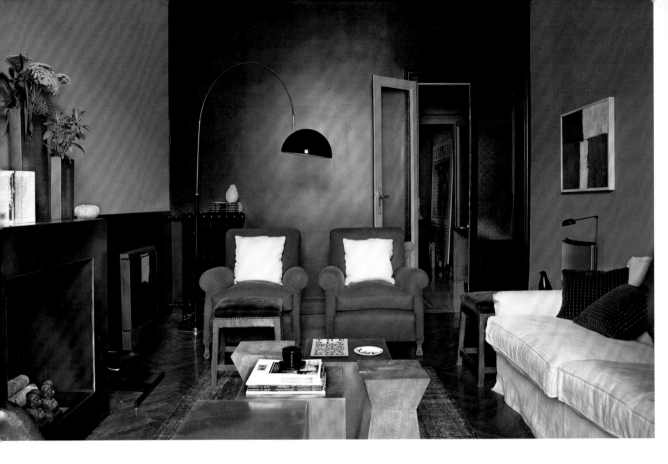

SPLURGE OR SAVE... *ARE EXPENSIVE PAINTS REALLY WORTH IT?*

ABOVE *The original features of this Milan apartment are enhanced by different shades of grey. The black lamp balances the white sofa and the cushions lead the eye across to the the mantelpiece and the vases and plants.*

Why is it that some greys are rich and opulent, while others just make your sitting room look like an office? Well, the difference between opulent and office is often to do with the amount of pigment in a particular shade.

Just as velvet feels more luxurious than cotton, so a paint rich in high-quality pigments will look deeper and richer on the wall. Designers will tell you that when it comes to grey the more expensive the paint the better, as it will have more pigment. And when there is a lot of pigment, explains stylist and TV host Emily Henderson, the paint isn't just a flat colour on the wall, but has a lot of 'movement'.

"That sounds crazy 'decorator-y'," Emily says, "but basically the more colours in a paint, the more subtly interesting it is – it's like secret texture. You can't stare at it and see the different colours, but instead you'll notice that it looks different in the morning than it does in the evening, and it changes so much based on what colours you put next to it."

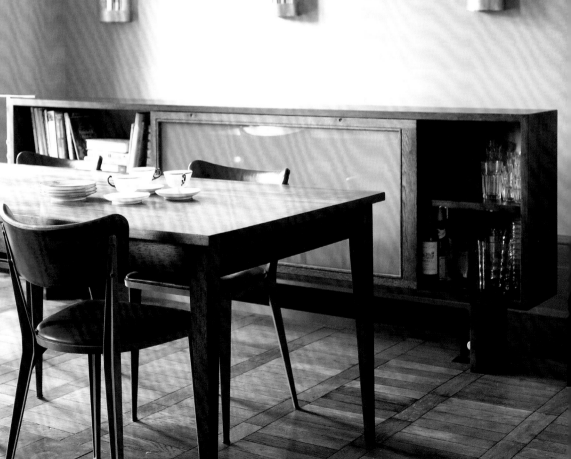

THIS PAGE *A blue-grey backdrop to lots of salvaged wood in a north-west facing kitchen in London makes for a restful and well-curated space. Try Dulux Monument Grey or Scree by Little Greene.*

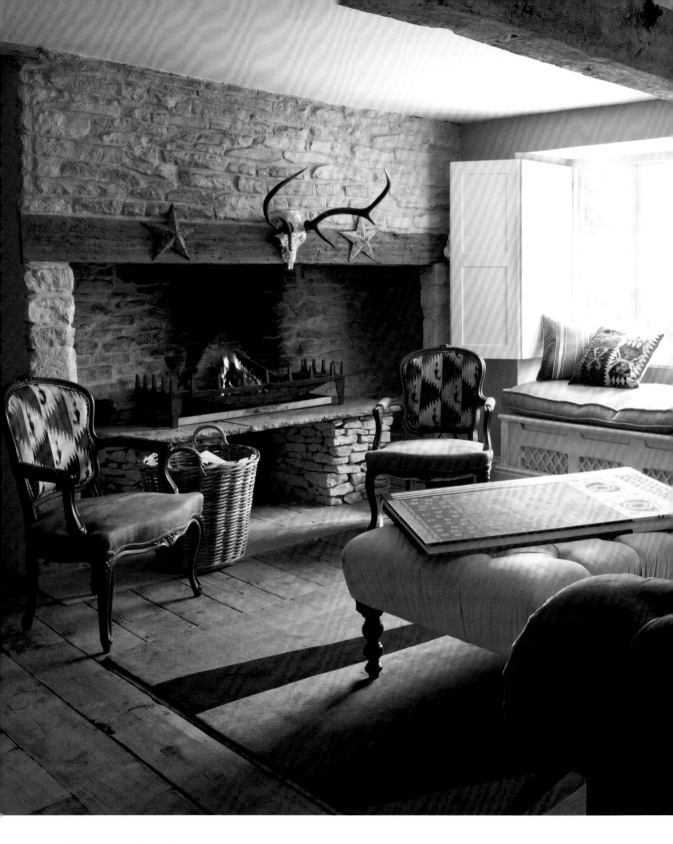

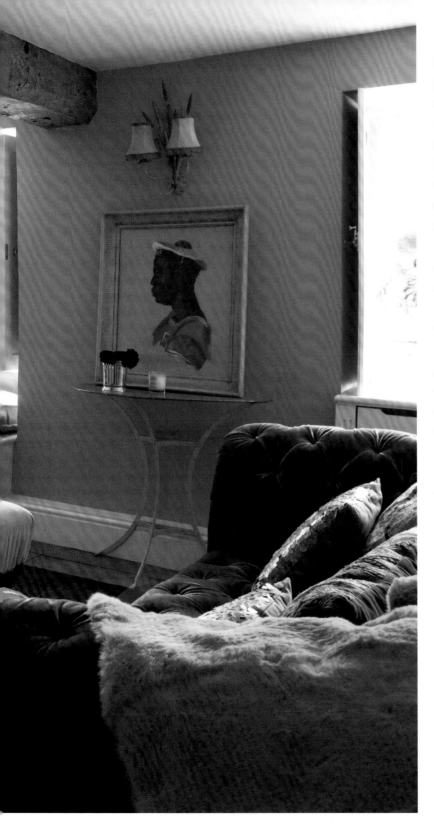

Designer Abigail Ahern says a flat grey can look depressing and that you must make sure you choose one with rich undertones that's made from natural pigments. "I can't rave about these pigments enough, as they're what give the beautiful nuances of colours and always make a hue that's more intriguing to the eye," she says.

David Mottershead, a trained chemist and the MD of Little Greene, says the more pigment in a paint, the better the depth of colour. "You might think grey is a non-colour, but in fact it contains a lot of different pigments and the proportion of red oxide to verdigris will have an effect on the other colours it will go with," he says. Which explains why you think you have found the perfect shade of grey in the tin yet later discover that it looks terrible with your purple sofa.

LEFT *This room is painted in Farrow & Ball's French Gray, which is a definite greeny grey, and the owners of this room have highlighted that with their choice of furnishings and accents of green and yellow throughout. Using pink or orange would have had the effect of subtly altering the colour of the walls.*

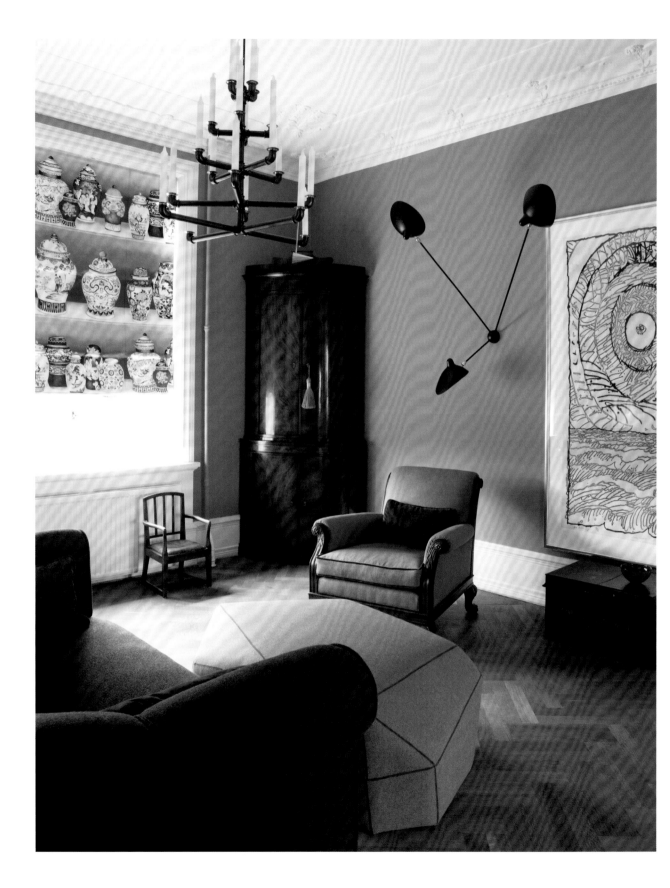

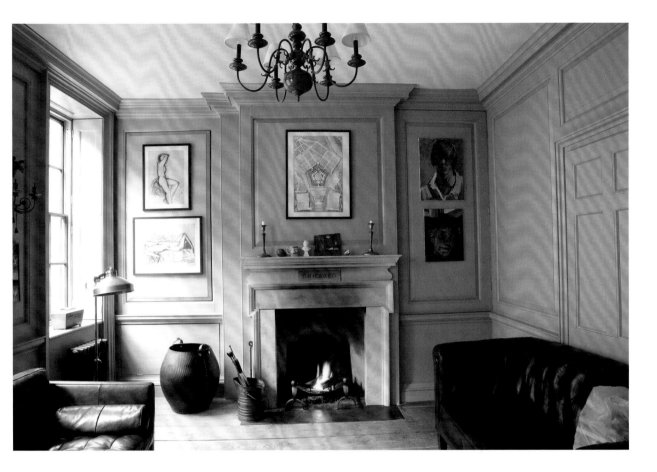

OPPOSITE *Antique furniture and a parquet floor work well with grey too. The black three-armed light and chandelier provide anchor points in this scheme. Try Plummet for a similar shade.*

ABOVE *Panelled walls look wonderful painted grey, which brings a more contemporary feel to an old building. Mix with modern furniture to create an interesting space.*

Grey is made up of lots of different pigments, which is how it becomes warm or cool. The Little Greene paint chart starts with cool shades on the left and works across to those with more ochre, which will be warmer. Urbane Grey has a lot of verdigris, so it will go with blue shades, for example, but Dolphin has a higher proportion of red oxide and looks better with colours from the pinker end of the spectrum.

Pigments are expensive, especially when it comes to violets, blues and reds. And this, in a nutshell, is why you can't really find an 'equivalent' (i.e. a less-expensive) version of expensive paints. Not only does the amount of pigment vary but, as so many different colours go into creating grey, without a recipe it's almost impossible to copy. That's why you can match a RAL colour, because you do have the recipe.

BELOW *A stack of clear glass jars filled with different shades of grey paint on a grey cupboard make for an unusual and eclectic decoration.*

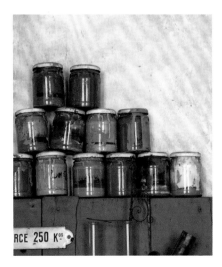

THIS PAGE AND OPPOSITE, CLOCKWISE FROM RIGHT *The grey stairs and darker grey architrave is a good example of layering shades of grey. See how the dark door frame highlights the lighter space beyond; A collection of grey candlesticks against a grey wall provides a sculptural still life; This kitchen has brushed aluminium doors, vintage blue and white tiles and dark grey paint to highlight the china. Try Dulux Monument Grey for a similar shade; Not all grey is paint; this bathroom is covered in salvaged fossil limestone, providing texture as well as colour.*

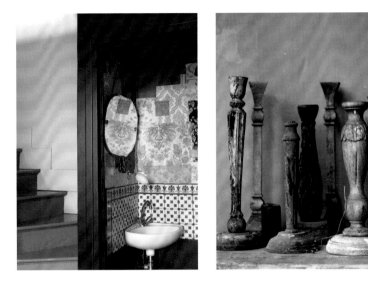

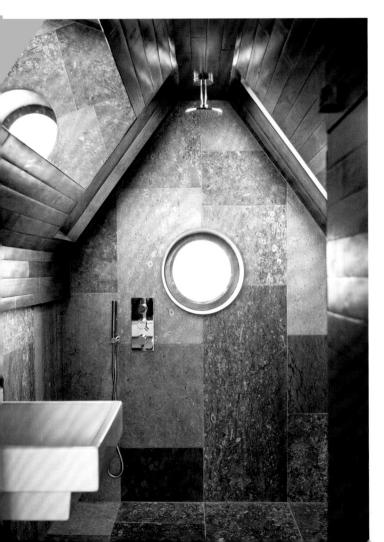

You can go to the paint mixing store and ask for a 'match', but (and I know people who have fallen foul of this) when you go back to buy more so that you can touch up scuffs, the colour probably won't be exactly the same because it wasn't created to exactly the same recipe. It won't match and you will have to repaint the whole wall. Be realistic; decide what you can afford to spend and research the colour accordingly. That way you won't end up staring at a pale imitation of what you wanted and wishing you had bought the real thing.

The codicil to this is that you should always buy the best that you can afford and budget accordingly. If buying expensive paint means you have to sit on a less-expensive sofa, then you will have to decide which matters more. But bear in mind that the walls, floors and lighting are the bone structure of a room. Get those right and, just as a top model can look amazing in a chainstore dress, so your inexpensive sofa can only improve when set against a grey canvas with clever lighting.

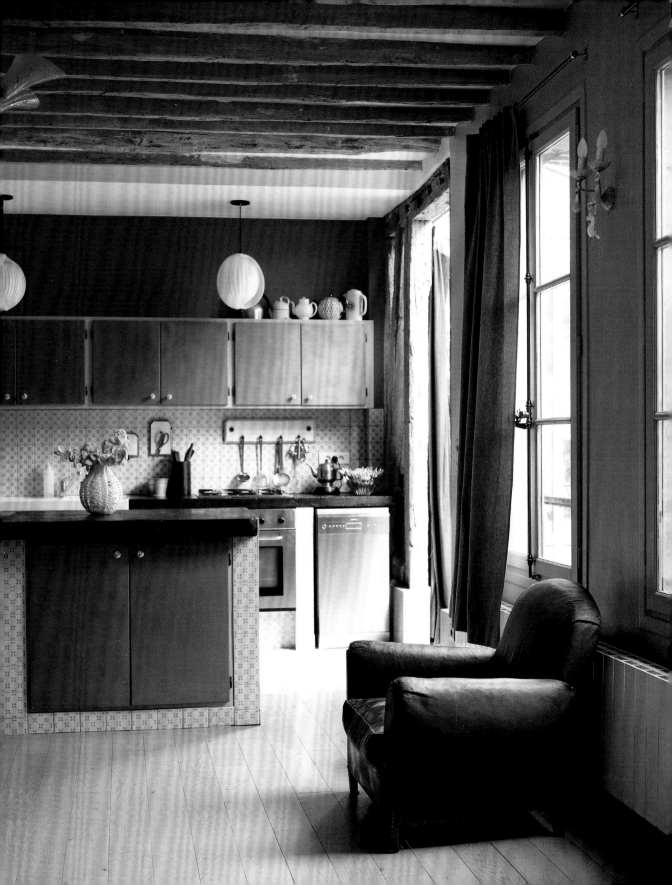

THIS PAGE *With a fireplace this striking it would be wrong not to highlight it, and the dark blue-grey paint works perfectly against the pale walls. Try Dulux Pearl Grey or Farrow & Ball Cornforth White for the walls.*

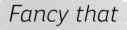

Fancy that

Legends are full of grey cats, grey bears and grey wolves, not to mention various ghostly grey ladies.

The venerable American daily newspaper The New York Times (established 1851) is sometimes referred to as 'The Gray Lady'.

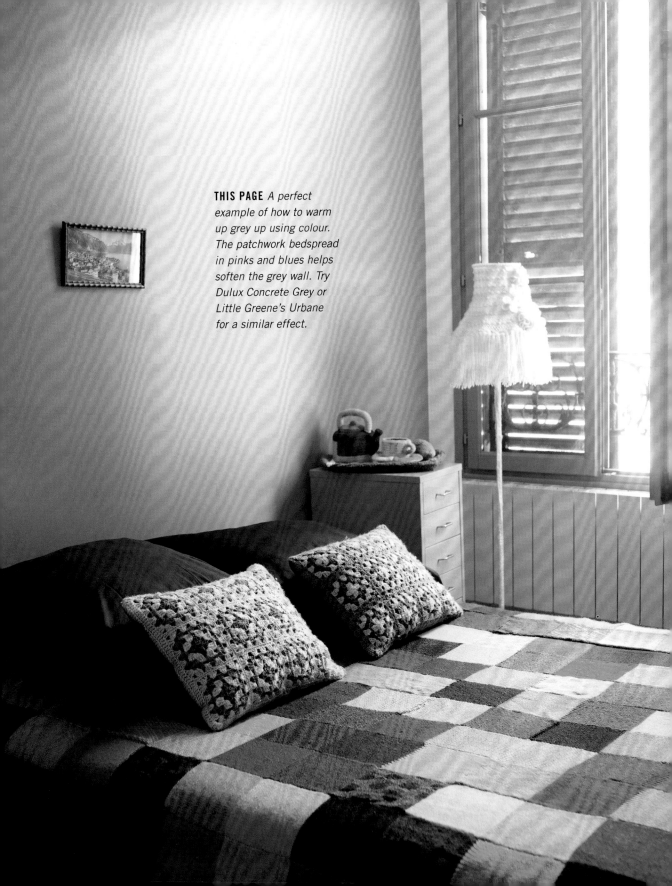

THIS PAGE *A perfect example of how to warm up grey up using colour. The patchwork bedspread in pinks and blues helps soften the grey wall. Try Dulux Concrete Grey or Little Greene's Urbane for a similar effect.*

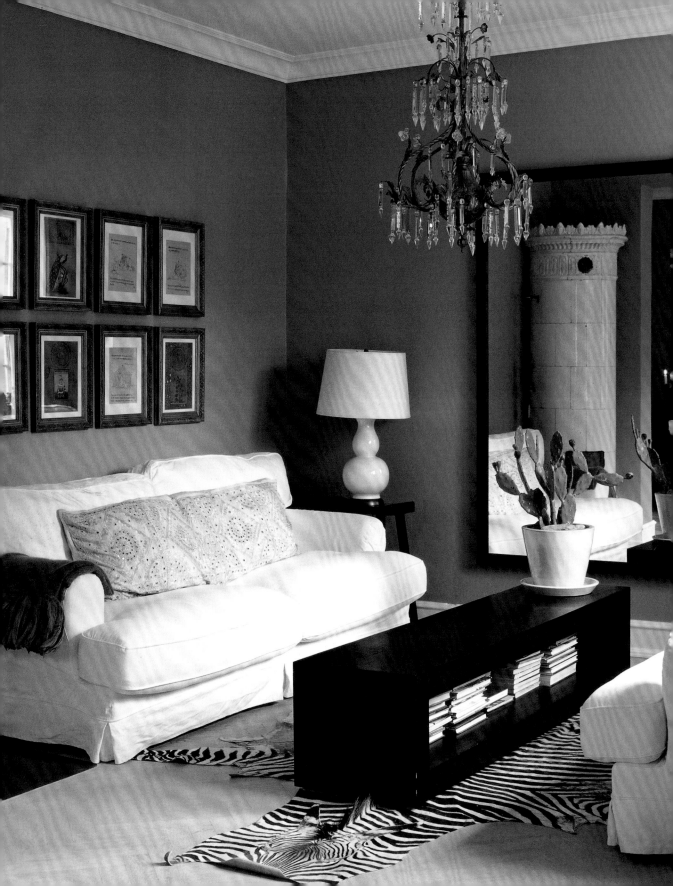

ECO
OR NOT?

Surely it's just a bit of pigment and some water – how bad can paint be? Cast your mind back to the days of using oil-based paints – remember how the odour of fresh paint would linger for days? This is because paint contains various solvents that, among other things, help it dry. The worst of these is formaldehyde, a volatile organic compound (VOC) and known carcinogen. VOCs are given out while paint dries and for up to five years afterwards.

OPPOSITE *In this Danish home, the restricted palette of grey, white and dark wood is not austere, thanks to the zebra rug and ornate chandelier.*

RIGHT *The dining room is the perfect place to experiment with a dark colour as you don't spend hours in there so can afford to be daring.*

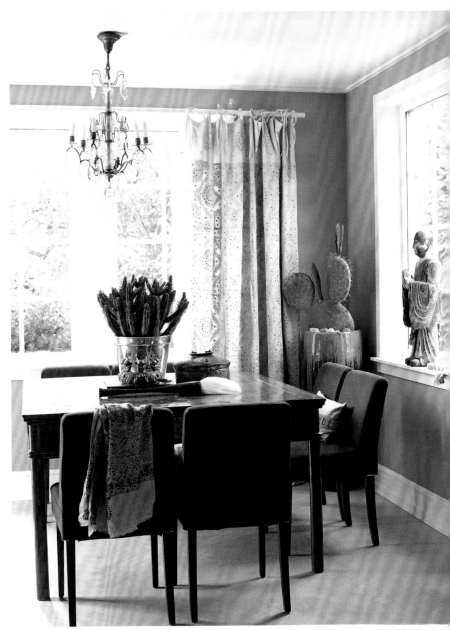

Since 2010 there have been laws limiting the amount of VOCs that can be used in paint, but as paint companies don't have to list their ingredients, we (the customer) still don't know exactly what we're buying. The good news is that you can now choose from an increasing range of low-VOC or VOC-free products. Farrow & Ball sells low-VOC paint and Benjamin Moore has a range of zero VOCs, as does Sherwin-Williams. Other low-VOC ranges include Edward Bulmer Pots of Paint, Marston & Langinger and Earthborn. Edward Bulmer believes that all companies should list their ingredients. "That way, you can make an informed choice. We try to be as clear as possible."

But that's just about the paint we're buying now. What about the stuff we've finished using? We buy around 300 million litres of paint every year in the UK, and it's estimated that around 50 million litres of it go unused or are just thrown away. The numbers are no less shocking in the US, where the Environmental Protection Agency calculated in 2007 that around 10 per cent of the 83 million gallons (313 million litres) sold annually are discarded.

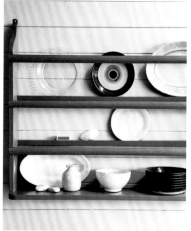

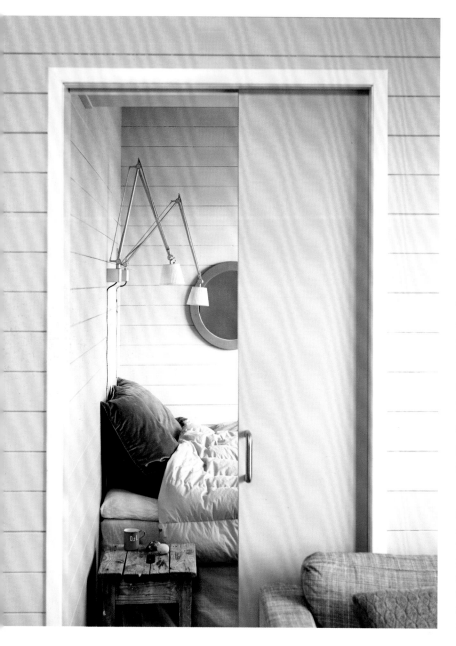

In 2002, a chemist named Keith Harrison decided to do something about this. Tired of being gently nagged by his wife to clear out the garage, he assumed it was possible to recycle paint and went to look for the nearest drop-off point. When he realized that there wasn't one, Keith spent the next two years developing a way to reprocess waste paint into high-grade emulsion. Newlife Paints launched in 2008 and, as well as selling its own range of Reborn paints, has collaborated with Mini Moderns on their environmentally responsible paint, which includes three greys; Concrete, Slate and Weathered Cedar.

ABOVE AND LEFT *Another house in Denmark, this time by the sea, where the owners have chosen a pale grey that looks almost white in bright sunlight. The dark grey shelves (above) and bedlinen anchor the space and stop it looking boring. Dulux Rock Salt would be a good match for this.*

THIS PAGE *In another shot from the same house, this is a perfect way to see how introducing some warmth in the shape of natural textiles – wood and rattan – have transformed this space into a cosy, welcoming area. That pale grey could otherwise be cold.*

Now that someone has started recycling paint, it seems like a blindingly obvious thing to do and you're left wondering why everyone wasn't already doing it. But it's not that simple. Paint is a complex mix of around 10 to 20 chemical components, so to be able to recycle it you need some chemical knowledge, says Keith. "We licence our process so that we train companies in the technology of how to produce a good and consistent quality paint from waste paint. One main problem is that the waste regulations are complex, and

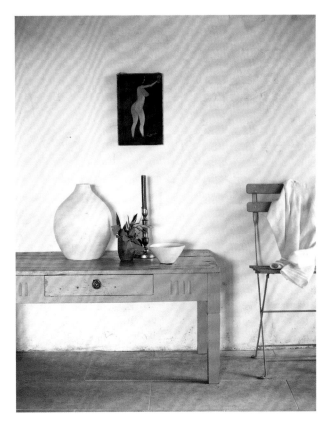

RIGHT *Old brown furniture can be given a new lease of life with a coat of paint.*

BELOW LEFT AND RIGHT *Half-painted walls are a current trend and, although common in houses with dado rails, actually look* *more modern if there is no such rail. The pink bedding brings a warmth to this rather concrete-like shade, while the taupey grey in the bathroom (try Elephant's Breath by Farrow & Ball) is echoed by the tiled floor and the bathtub.*

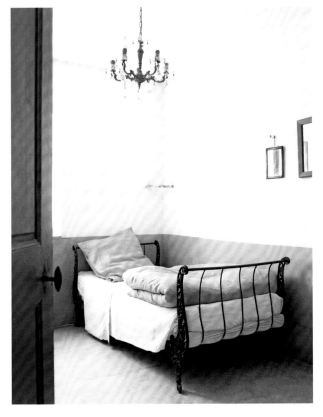

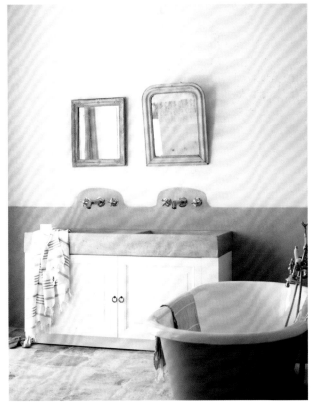

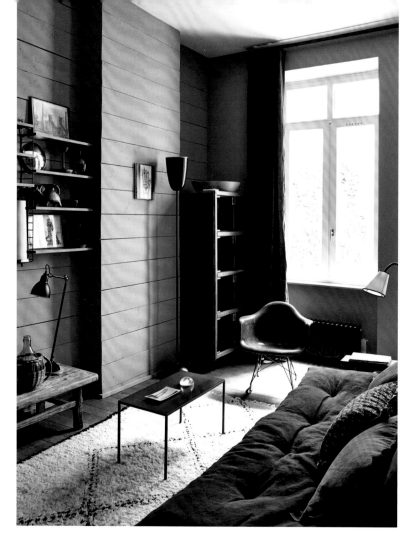

so are the manufacturing regulations, and to recycle paint you need to be able to handle both sets of regulations."

Keith also mentions that the first paint he ever recycled was grey and it's still on his bathroom wall now. "We have probably made 10 to 15 versions of grey, and we do bespoke versions too. Recently. I made a special non-slip dark grey floor exterior grade paint for a colleague." He continues, "When we started out, grey was not a popular colour and wasn't really found in the waste stream. However, it began to rise in popularity some years before a certain book came out and has continued to rise ever since."

OPPOSITE *The large cream rug brings a little light to the mix but the combination of navy upholstery and grey walls is unusual and luxurious.*

ABOVE, RIGHT AND FAR RIGHT *These pictures are of a tiny pied-à-terre in an old house in France. The owners have kept the colour palette simple throughout, but instead of falling into the trap of painting a small space white to try and make it look bigger, they have embraced its size and gone dark. Lots of natural wood also works hard to bring another layer of interest. Try Little Greene Mid Lead for a similar shade and remember that you can easily change cushions and rugs to freshen up the look.*

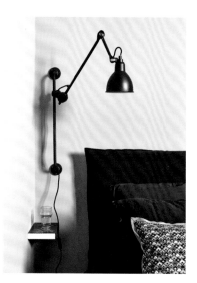

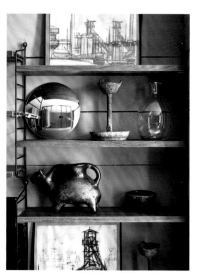

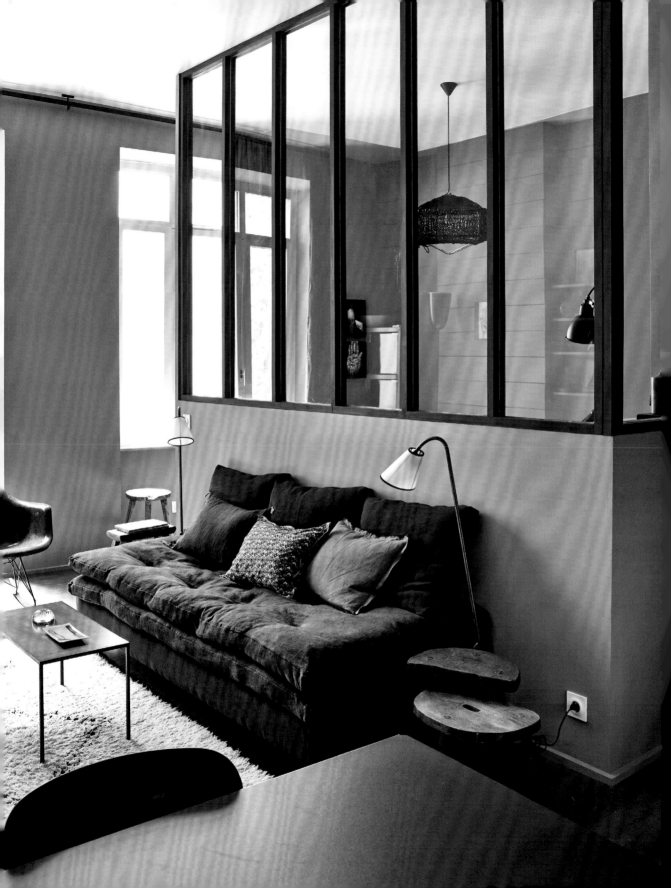

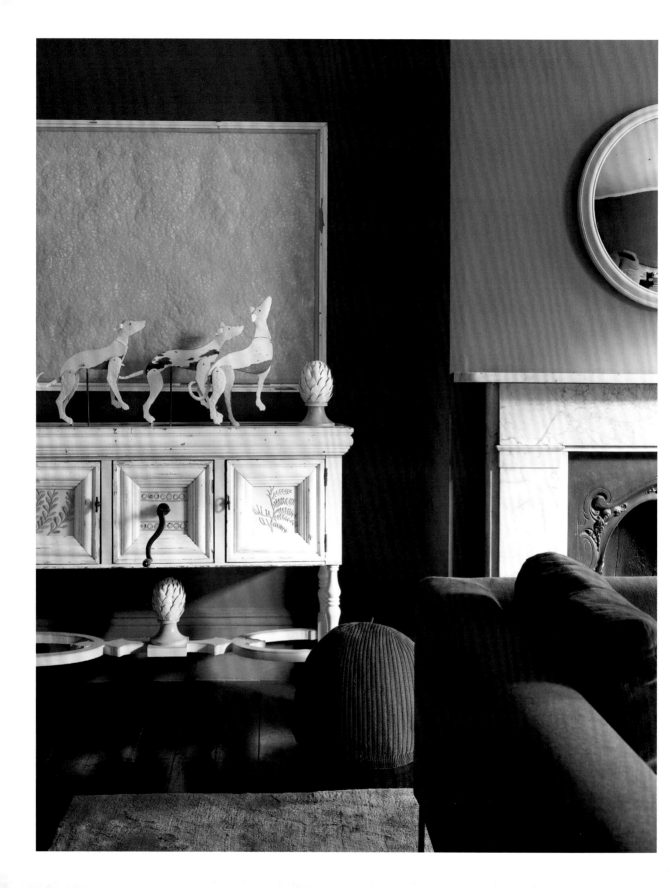

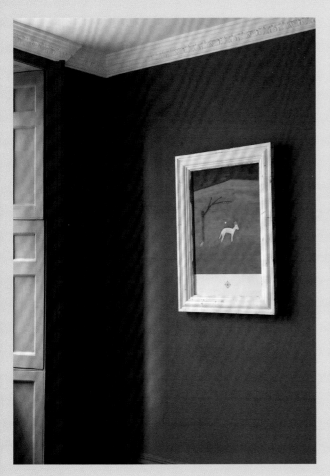

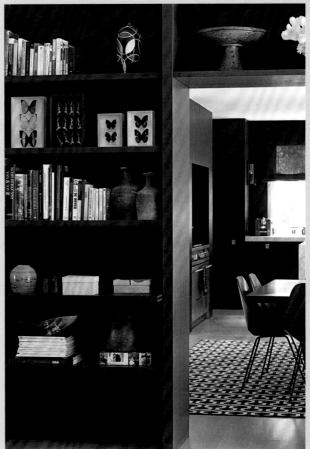

OPPOSITE AND THIS PAGE *The power of dark grey. Opposite, the dark walls and sofa almost match, but the dashes of pink, white and blue bring a sense of fun; A painting really pops against the dark wall. Against white paint, a picture would have less impact or need a couple more to create a statement; Go as dark as you dare – this shelving makes works of art of everything on display, thanks to the dark walls. Relief comes from the monochrome rug and wooden floor in the kitchen beyond. For a good match, try Farrow & Ball Railings.*

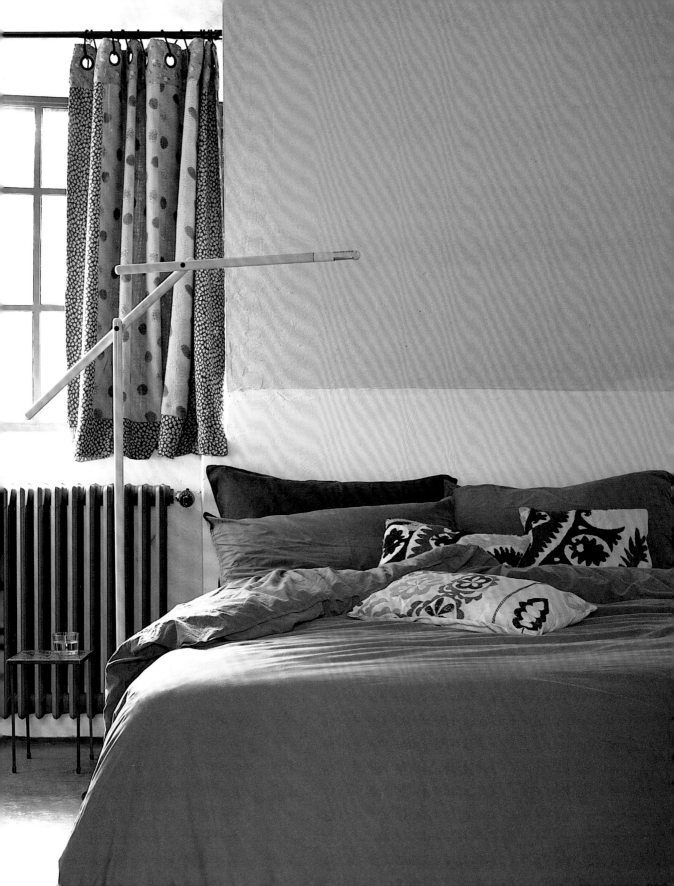

PAINTING BY NUMBERS

- Of the 132 shades on the Farrow & Ball colour chart, at least 20 could be classified as greys – a 10 per cent increase in the past seven years.

- Dulux sales of grey paint have increased by 4.1 per cent since 2012.

- Benjamin Moore has 360 shades of grey paint, according to Hannah Yeo, the company's colour manager.

- Little Greene has created an entire capsule collection of 28 shades of grey ranging from Loft White to Chimney Brick.

- If you stick 'grey paint' into Google, it comes up with around 98,000,000 results in 0.4 seconds.

- There is some dispute about how many different shades of grey the human eye can perceive. It has been claimed that it's 500, but a recent report from the University of Cincinnati suggested that it's actually closer to 30.

THIS PAGE AND OPPOSITE *In these rooms, a grey render, rather than paint, has been used on the walls, which gives a more natural finish. The overall effect is one of warm, rustic modernity.*

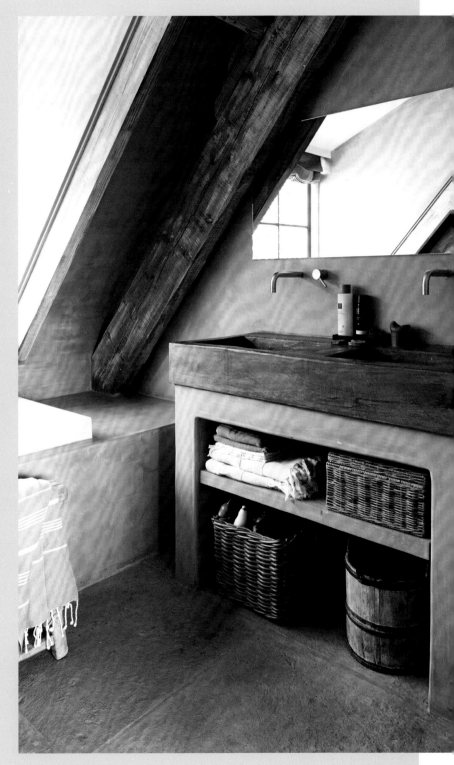

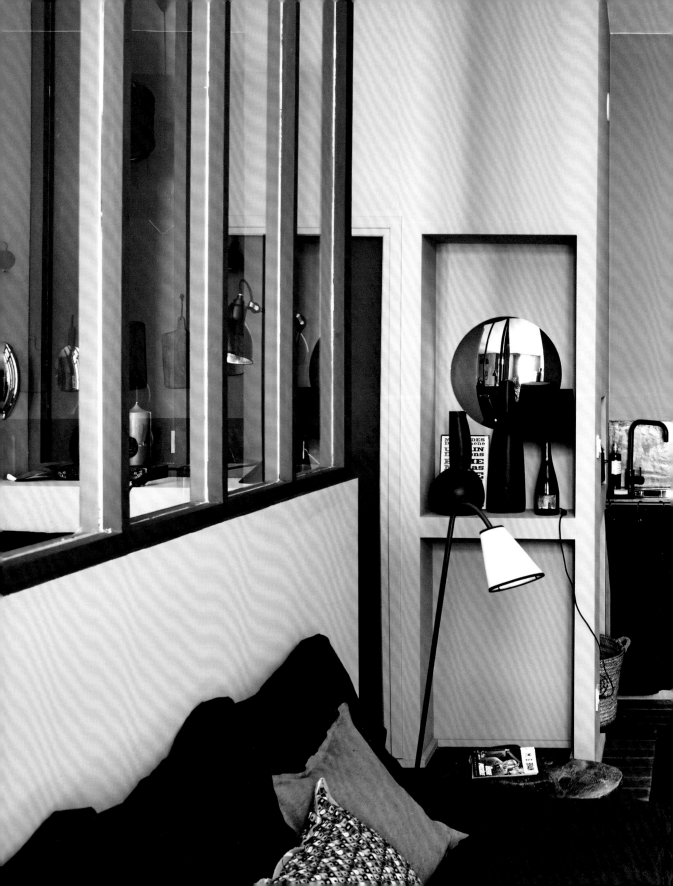

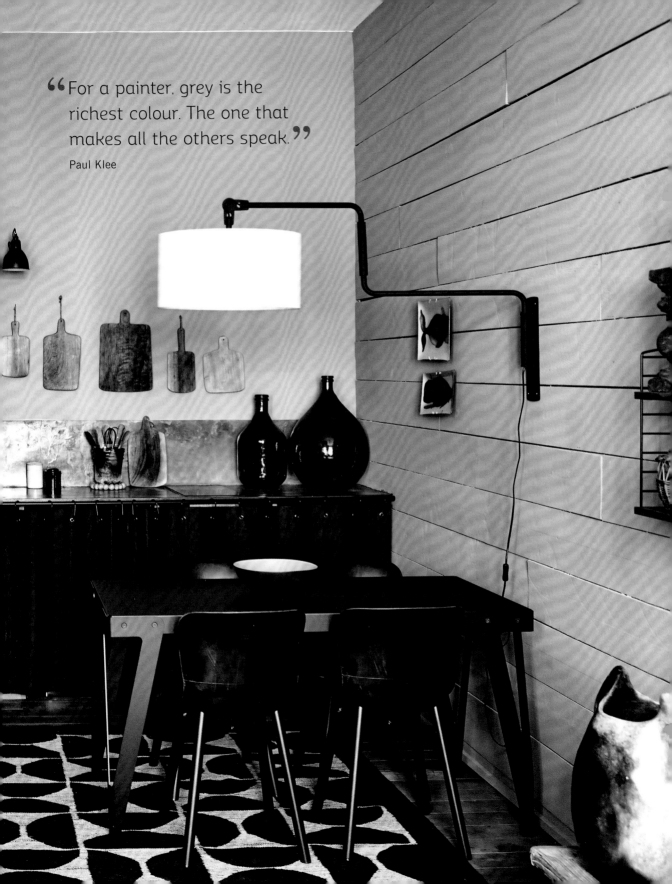

> "For a painter, grey is the richest colour. The one that makes all the others speak."
>
> Paul Klee

INDEX

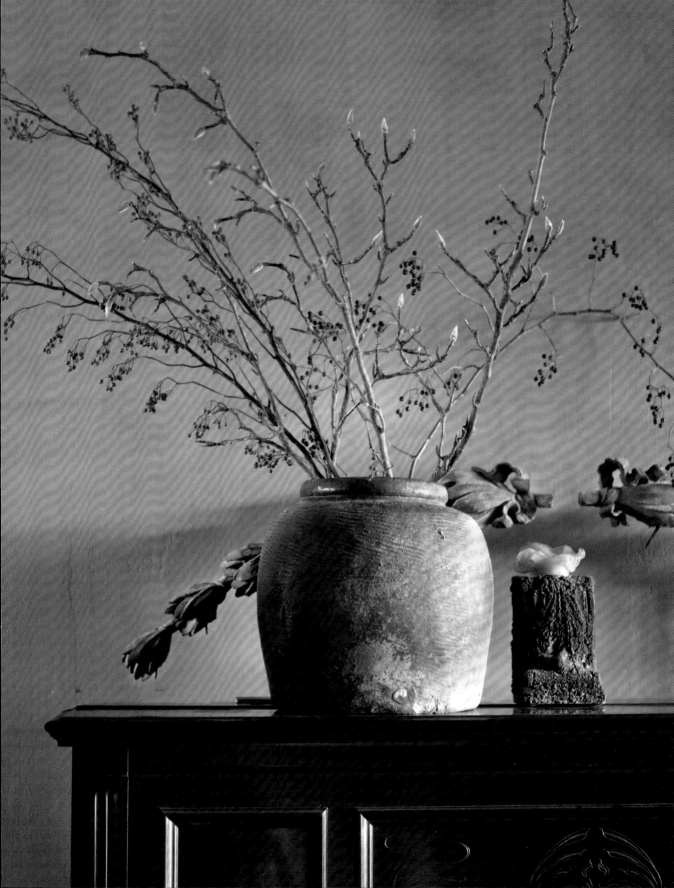

PICTURE CREDITS

Key: ph = photographer; **a** = above; **b** = below; **r** = right; **l** = left; **c** = centre.

1 Bruno et Michèle Viard, location-en-luberon.com, ph Polly Wreford **2** The home of Birgitte and Henrik Moller Kastrup in Denmark, ph Rachel Whiting **3l** The home of the designer Agnès Emery of Emery & Cie in the Medina in Marrakech, ph Katya de Grunwald **3c & 3r** The Norfolk home of the designer Petra Boase, ph Debi Treloar **4** photography and styling by Hans Blomquist **5** The home of interior journalist and blogger Jill Macnair in London, ph Rachel Whiting **6** Robert Young, Robert Young Architecture and Interiors www.ryarch.com, ph Earl Carter **7** ph Paul Massey **8a** Stylist Karen Harrison's house in East Sussex. Available for photoshoots, please contact Emma Davies on 07734 617639. Ph Jan Baldwin **8b** The home of stylist Twig Hutchinson in London, ph Polly Wreford **9** The home of Chris van Eldik and Wendy Jansen of J.O.B. Interieurs, ph Lisa Cohen **10** The home of designer Agnès Emery of Emery & Cie in the Medina in Marrakech, ph Katya de Grunwald **11al** The home of Jonathan Sela and Megan Schoenbachler, ph Catherine Gratwicke **11r** The family home of Rebecca Proctor in Cornwall www.futuristicblog.com, ph Rachel Whiting **11b** ph Simon Brown **12–13** Robert Young, Robert Young Architecture & Interiors www.ryarch.com, ph Earl Carter **14–15** The home of Birgitte and Henrik Moller Kastrup in Denmark, ph Rachel Whiting **16** The home of Maria and Frank in Southern Germany, interior design by Barbara G, ph Jan Baldwin **17l** The home of photographer and designer Paul Massey (paulmassey.me) **17r** Judith Kramer, owner of webshop Juudt.com, ph Polly Wreford **18a** www.les-sardines.com, ph Claire Richardson **18b** The home of Karina, Victor and George Bjerregaard Chen in Denmark, ph Jan Baldwin **19** Chateau de Christin, Chambres d'Hotes de Luxe, Reception - Seminaires, ph Claire Richardson **20** A family home in west London by Webb Architects and Cave Interiors, ph Polly Wreford **21** Bruno et Michèle Viard, location-en-luberon.com, ph Polly Wreford **22a** La Maison Pujol B&B near Carcassonne, France, owned by Aurélie and René Mosser, www.lamaisonpujol.net, ph Debi Treloar **22bl** The home of artist and antiques dealer and interior designer Monique Meij-Beekman in the Netherlands, ph Debi Treloar **22br** The home of Chris van Eldik and Wendy Jansen of J.O.B. Interieurs, ph Lisa Cohen **23** The Paris apartment of Audrey Chabert, designed by architect Sylvie Cahen, ph Rachel Whiting **24** The home of designer Marijke van Nunen, ph Lisa Cohen **25** The home of antiques dealer and interior designer Oliver Gustav in Copenhagen, ph Debi Treloar **26** Place Farmhouse, available for location shoot rental through www.beachstudios.co.uk, ph Polly Wreford **27** Swan House B&B in Hastings, wallpaper by Melissa White (www.fairlyte.co.uk), ph Claire Richardson **28–29** www.stylexclusief.nl, ph Catherine Gratwicke **30** The home in Lewes of Justin and Heidi Francis, owner of Flint www.flintcollection.com, ph Polly Wreford **31** Elizabeth Machin's Norfolk cottage, ph Jan Baldwin **32** The London home of Steven and Jane Collins, owner of Sixty 6 boutique, ph Andrew Wood **33al** The house of Eifion and Amanda Griffiths of Melin Tregwynt in Wales, ph Claire Richardson **33ar** The home of designers Piet and Karin Boon near Amsterdam, www.pietboon.nl, ph Lisa Cohen **33bl** The Norfolk family home of the designer Petra Boase, ph Debi Treloar **33br** www.beachstudios.co.uk, ph Polly Wreford **34–37a** The London home of James Soane and Christopher Ash of Project Orange, ph Jan Baldwin **37bl** The home of Tim Rundle and Glynn Jones, ph Debi Treloar **37br** The home of Ashlyn Gibson, founder of children's concept store Olive Loves Alfie, interior stylist/writer and children's fashion stylist, ph Rachel Whiting **38l** ph Hans Blomquist **38r** The home of film director Christina Höglund in Österlen, Sweden, ph Debi Treloar **39** The home of Rose Hammick and Andrew Treverton (www.marmoraroad.de) ph Polly Wreford **40a** and **41** New Cross location available for location shoot rental from www.beachstudios.co.uk, ph Polly Wreford **40ar** and **40b** Varden Street location available to hire through www.lightlocations.co.uk, ph Polly Wreford **42** The home of Rose Hammick and Andrew Treverton (www.marmoraroad.co.uk), ph Polly Wreford **43** ph James Merrell **44–45** The London home of Conrad Roeber and David Townsend of interior design practice Schubart Masters, ph Jan Baldwin **46** Les Trois Salons, Uzes, creators and owners Charmaine and Paul Jack, ph Claire Richardson **47a** The Paris home of the architect Joseph Dirand, ph Pia Ulin **47b** The Milan home of Marzio Cavanna, ph Pia Ulin **48a, 48bl** and **49** Judith Kramer, owner of webshop Juudt.com, ph Polly Wreford **48br** The Paris home of interior designer Sarah Lavoine, ph Polly Wreford **50l** The London home of James Soane and Christopher Ash of Project Orange, ph Jan Baldwin **50r** The Milan home of Marzio Cavanna, ph Pia Ulin **51** The home of the stylist Ingeborg Wolf, ph Pia Ulin **52al** Bruno et Michèle Viard, location-en-luberon.com, ph Polly Wreford **52ar** The Greenwich home of Alison Hill and John Taylor, ph Jan Baldwin **52bl** The home of the designer Agnès Emery of Emery & Cie in Marrakech, ph Katya de Grunwald **52br** The home of Jocie Sinauer, owner of Red Chair on Warren St in Hudson, New York, ph Anna Williams **53** www.chambresenville.be in Brussels, ph Anna Williams **54–55** The home of the stylist Ingeborg Wolf, ph Pia Ulin **56** The home of artist and antiques dealer and interior designer Monique Meij-Beekman in the Netherlands, ph Debi Treloar **57** Judith Kramer, owner of webshop Juudt.com, ph Polly Wreford **58–59** The home of fashion designer Virginie Denny and artist Alfonso Vallès, ph Debi Treloar **60–61** L'Atelier d'Archi – Isabelle Juy – www.latelierdarchi.fr, ph Polly Wreford **62l** www.janconstantine.com, ph Paul Massey **62r–63** Long Farm, the home of architect Lucy Marston in Suffolk, ph Polly Wreford **64al** The home of the interior decorator Caroline Van Thillo in Belgium, ph Polly Wreford **64ar** The home of antiques dealer and interior designer Oliver Gustav in Copenhagen, ph Debi Treloar **64bl** The home of Family Voors in the Netherlands designed by Karin Draaijer, ph Polly Wreford **64br** The family home of Sacha Paisley in Sussex, designed by Arior Design, ph Polly Wreford **65** The Linen Shed, boutique B&B near Whitstable, Kent, UK (www.linenshed.com), ph Catherine Gratwicke **66** The home of Chris van Eldik and Wendy Jansen of J.O.B. Interieurs, ph Lisa Cohen **67l** The home of antiques dealer and interior designer Oliver Gustav in Copenhagen, ph Debi Treloar **67r** A family home in west London by Webb Architects and Cave Interiors, ph Polly Wreford **68a** The cabin of Hanne Borge and her family in Norway, ph Catherine Gratwicke **68bl** The home of antiques dealer and interior designer Oliver Gustav in Copenhagen, ph Debi Treloar **68br** The home of Chris van Eldik and Wendy Jansen of J.O.B. Interieurs, ph Lisa Cohen **69** The Paris apartment of Philippe Model, ph Chris Everard **70** L'Atelier d'Archi – Isablle Juy – www.latelierdarchi.fr, ph Polly Wreford **71** Judith Kramer, owner of webshop Juudt.com, ph Polly Wreford **72–73** 'La Maison du College Royal', ph Jan Baldwin **74–75** The London home of designer Helen Ellery, ph Jan Baldwin **76–77** The London home of Conrad Roeber and David Townsend of interior design practice Schubart Masters, ph Jan Baldwin **78** www.sophieconran.com, ph Jan Baldwin **79** Chris Dyson Architects, ph Jan Baldwin **80** The Milan home of Marzio Cavanna, ph Pia Ulin **81** La Villa des Ombelles, the family home of Jean-Marc Dimanche Chairman of V.I.T.R.I.O.L. agency (www.vitriol-factory.com), ph Debi Treloar **82–83a** The home of Family Voors in the Netherlands designed by Karin Draaijer, ph Polly Wreford **83bl** Judith Kramer, owner of webshop Juudt.com, ph Polly Wreford **83br** The cabin of Hanne Borge and her family in Norway, ph Catherine Gratwicke **84al** Designed by McLean Quinlan Architects, ph Christopher Drake **84ar** The Paris home of interior designer Sarah Lavoine, ph Polly Wreford **84bl** The Milan home of Marzio Cavanna, ph Pia Ulin **84br** Stylist Karen Harrison's house in East Sussex (Available for photoshoots, please contact Emma Davies on 07734 617639), ph Jan Baldwin **85** The home of Hanne Borge in Norway, ph Catherine Gratwicke **86–87** Alison Hill and John Taylor's home in Greenwich, ph Jan Baldwin **88–89** The home and studio of Julian Stair in London, taken from the book *Simple Home* by Mark and Sally Bailey (www.baileyshome.com), ph Debi Treloar **90l** The home of Tim Rundle and Glynn Jones, ph Debi Treloar **90r–91** Les Trois Salons, Uzes – creators and owners Charmaine and Paul Jack, ph Claire Richardson **92** ph Polly Wreford **93al** The home of interior designer Eva Gnaedinger in Switzerland, ph Jan Baldwin **93ar** The family home of the stylist Anja Koops and chef Alain Parry in Amsterdam, ph Polly Wreford **93b** The home in London of Abigail Ahern (www.atelierabigailahern.com), ph Lisa Cohen **94** The London home of Conrad Roeber and David Townsend of interior design practice Schubart Masters, ph Jan Baldwin **95** The cabin of Hanne Borge and her family in Norway, ph Catherine Gratwicke **96** The family home of Alison Smith in Brighton, ph Polly Wreford **97l** ph Debi Treloar **97r** The family home of Johan Gjendem and Vibeke Rognan in Oslo, designed by architect Knut Hjeltnes, ph Catherine Gratwicke **98–99** 'La Maison du College Royal', ph Jan Baldwin **100l** The London home of Steven and Jane Collins, owner of Sixty 6 boutique, ph Andrew Wood **100r–101** New Cross location available for shoot rental through www.beachstudios.co.uk, ph Polly Wreford **102** Varden Street location available to hire through www.lightlocations.co.uk, ph Polly Wreford **103** Jo Berryman's home in London, ph Jan Baldwin **104** The home of Eifion and Amanda Griffiths of Melin Tregwynt in Wales, ph Claire Richardson **105al** The home of George Lamb in London, designed by Maria Speake of Retrouvius, ph Debi Treloar **105ar** Madeleine Rogers of Mibo, ph Debi Treloar **105bl** www.stylexclusief.nl, ph Catherine Gratwicke **105br** The home of designer Laure Vial du Chatenetof Maison Caumont Paris, ph Jan Baldwin **106a** The home of James Russell and Hannah Plumb, the artists behind JAMESPLUMB (www.jamesplumb.co.uk), ph Debi Treloar **106b** The home of designer Marijke van Nunen, ph Lisa Cohen **107** The home of Victoria and Stephen Fordham, designed by Sarah Delaney, in London, ph Polly Wreford **108** The home of Sophie Lambert, owner of Au Temps des Cerises in France, ph Jan Baldwin **109** Swan House B&B in Hastings, wallpaper by Melissa White (www.fairlyte.co.uk), ph Claire Richardson **110–111a** The home of Karina, Victor and George Bjerregaard Chen in Denmark, ph Jan Baldwin **111b** The London home of Conrad Roeber and David Townsend of interior design practice Schubart Masters, ph Jan Baldwin **112** The home of Karina, Victor and George Bjerregaard Chen in Denmark, ph Jan Baldwin **113** The Milan home of Marzio Cavanna, ph Pia Ulin **114** L'Atelier d'Archi – Isabelle Juy – www.latelierdarchi.fr, ph Polly Wreford **115a** The home of artist Binny Mathews and architect Stuart Martin in Dorset, ph Jan Baldwin **115bl** The cabin of Hanne Borge and her family in Norway, ph Catherine Gratwicke **115br** The Copenhagen home of June and David, ph Polly Wreford **116–117** The home of the decorator Bunny Turner of www.turnerpocock.co.uk, ph Polly Wreford **118l** Cathie Curran Architects, ph Polly Wreford **118r–119** The home of artist and antiques dealer and interior designer Monique Meij-Beekman in the Netherlands, ph Debi Treloar **120** and **121b** La Villa des Ombelles, the family home of Jean-Marc Dimanche Chairman of V.I.T.R.I.O.L. agency www.vitriol-factory.com, ph Debi Treloar **121a** The house of Catherine Vindevogel-Debal, owner of Tessuti, in Kortrijk, Belgium, kitchen designed by Filip Van Bever, ph Jan Baldwin **122l** www.aureliemathigot.com, ph Debi Treloar **122r–123** ph Debi Treloar **124al** and **bl** The home of artist and antiques dealer and interior designer Monique Meij-Beekman in the Netherlands, ph Debi Treloar **124ar** Judith Kramer, owner of webshop Juudt.com, ph Polly Wreford **124br** www.chambresenville.be in Brussels, ph Anna Williams **125** The home of interior decorator Caroline Van Thillo in Belgium, ph Polly Wreford **126–127** The London home of Graham Noakes of Osborne & Little, ph Claire Richardson **128** An apartment in Lyon, France, designed by Stéphane Garotin and Pierre Emmanuel Martin of Maison Hand, ph Rachel Whiting **129** Wynchelse, designed by Dave Coote and Atlanta Bartlett, available for holiday lets and location photography from www.beachstudios.co.uk, ph Polly Wreford **130a** www.stylexclusief.nl, ph Catherine Gratwicke **130b** The family home of Johan Gjendem and Vibeke Rognan in Oslo, designed by the architect Knut Hjeltnes, ph Catherine Gratwicke **131** The family home of Gina Portman of Folk at Home www.folkathome.com, ph Catherine Gratwicke **132** The home of artist and antiques dealer and interior designer Monique Meij-Beekman in the Netherlands, ph Debi Treloar **133** The cabin of Hanne Borge and her family in Norway, ph Catherine Gratwicke **134l** The family home of Sacha Paisley in Sussex, designed by Arior Design, ph Polly Wreford **134r** The home of antiques dealer and interior designer Oliver Gustav in Copenhagen, ph Debi Treloar **135** The home of Karina, Victor and George Bjerregaard Chen in Denmark, ph Jan Baldwin **136** Bruno et Michèle Viard, location-en-luberon.com, ph Polly Wreford **137** The Barton's seaside home in West Sussex, www.thedodo.co.uk, ph Paul Massey **138** The London home of interior designer Jo Berryman (joberryman.com), ph Jan Baldwin **139a** The home of the designer Agnès Emery of Emery & Cie in Marrakech, ph Katya de Grunwald **139b** ph Debi Treloar **140** Wendy Jansen and Chris Van Eldik, owners of J.O.B. Interieur's housein Wijk bij Duurstede, The Netherlands, ph Jan Baldwin **141al** The family home of the stylist Anja Koops and chef Alain Parry in Amsterdam, ph Polly Wreford **141ar** The cabin of Hanne Borge and her family in Norway, ph Catherine Gratwicke **141bl** The home of antiques dealer and interior designer Oliver Gustav in Copenhagen, ph Debi Treloar **141br** The family home of Clare Checkland and Ian Harding in Fife, ph Catherine Gratwicke **142** The London home of designer Helen Ellery, ph Jan Baldwin **143a** The London home of Graham Noakes of Osborne & Little, ph Claire Richardson **143b** 'The Folly' by Joanna Berryman. For interior design commissions please contact Joanna at joberryman.com. ph Jan Baldwin **144–145** The cabin of Hanne Borge and her family in Norway, ph Catherine Gratwicke **146** The home of Marzio Cavanna in Milan, ph Pia Ulin **147** The London home of Guy and Natasha Hills, designed by Maria Speake of Retrouvius, ph Debi Treloar **148–149** 'The Folly' by Joanna Berryman. For interior design commissions please contact Joanna at joberryman.com, ph Jan Baldwin **150** Ben Pentreath's house in Dorset, ph Jan Baldwin **151a** Chris Dyson Architects, ph Jan Baldwin **151b** Vox Populi, the studio of the artist/designer Pascale Palun, in Avignon, ph Debi Treloar **152al**, **153** and **155** www.aureliemathigot.com, ph Debi Treloar **152ar** The home of artist and antiques dealer and interior designer Monique Meij-Beekman in the Netherlands, ph Debi Treloar **152b** The London apartment of Retrouvius owners, Adam Hills and Maria Speake, ph Debi Treloar **154** The London home of Rose Hammick and Andrew Treverton, www.marmoraroad.co.uk, ph Polly Wreford **156–157** The home of Lars Wiberg of Pour Quoi in Copenhagen, ph Lisa Cohen **158–159** The home of Birgitte and Henrik Moller Kastrup in Denmark, ph Rachel Whiting **160** Robert Young, Robert Young Architecture & Interiors www.ryarch.com, ph Earl Carter **161a** The home of Charmaine and Paul Jack, Belvezet, France, ph Claire Richardson **161bl** Bruno et Michèle Viard, location-en-luberon.com, ph Polly Wreford **161br** The home of Constant Tedder in Italy, Interior Design by Alexander Waterworth Interiors and Architects Tully Filmer and Giovanni Musa, ph Polly Wreford **162–163** An apartment in Lyon, France, designed by Stéphane Garotin and Pierre Emmanuel Martin of Maison Hand, ph Rachel Whiting **164–165al** ph Polly Wreford **165ar** The home of the interior decorator Caroline Van Thillo in Belgium, ph Polly Wreford **166** Bea B&B owned by Bea Mombaers in Knokke-Le Zoute, Belgium (www.bea-bb.com), ph Anna Williams **167** www.stylexclusief.nl, ph Catherine Gratwicke **168–169** An apartment in Lyon, France, designed by Stéphane Garotin and Pierre Emmanuel Martin of Maison Hand, ph Rachel Whiting **171** The home of artist and antiques dealer and interior designer Monique Meij-Beekman in the Netherlands, ph Debi Treloar **176** photography and styling by Hans Blomquist.

SOURCES

ABIGAIL AHERN
12–14 Essex Road
London N1 8LN
+44 (0)20 7354 8181
www.abigailahern.com
Faux botanicals, furnishings and textiles, all in a luxurious, moody palette that's heavy on the grey. The paint range contains several luxurious, velvety greys, from steely Madison to Cinder, a warm grey with purple undertones, and calming Fog.

AMARA
www.amara.com
High-end online store with an enormous range of stock that is added to on a daily basis.

BAUWERK COLOUR
www.bauwerkcolour.co.uk
Exterior and interior lime paints made with clay, minerals and natural pigments for a soft, textured finish. There are several sumptuous shades of grey, from Mist to Paperbark, Slate and Juniper. Visit the website for advice on chasing the perfect grey.

CANVAS HOME
www.canvashomestore.com
This US store offers simple and stylish tableware, upholstered furniture and soft furnishings in shades of grey and other neutrals.

COX AND COX
www.coxandcox.co.uk
There must be 50 shades here – look out for their velvet quilts and café chairs, although some of the rugs are gorgeous too.

DEBENHAMS
www.debenhams.com
Look out for the Abigail Ahern collection, especially the animal lights.

DULUX
www.dulux.co.uk
More grey shades than you can shake a stick at...but their handy Ideas section and the colour finder takes away some of the guesswork.

DESIGN VINTAGE
www.designvintage.co.uk
A carefully curated collection of vintage and contemporary, there are warm, soft colours and lots of monochrome textiles.

EARTHBORN PAINTS
www.earthbornpaints.co.uk
Environmentally friendly paints including Claypaint, a clay-based breathable emulsion with a tactile chalky finish in subtle shades.

FARROW & BALL
www.farrow-ball.com
Water-based, low-VOC paints in a range of subtle shades with intriguing names. Visit their website for plenty of advice on choosing the perfect shade of grey for your space.

FERM LIVING
www.fermliving.com
Scandinavian designs with lots of simple clear graphics that reflect the background of its Danish founder Trine Andersen.

FINE NORDIC
www.finenordic.co.uk
Stick grey into the search engine and it comes back with over 600 items. That ought to be enough for even the most hardened grey-o-phile.

FOLKLORE
www.folklorehome.com
Simple and functional goods made from natural materials.

FRENCH CONNECTION
www.frenchconnection.com/home
UK fashion chain that has branched out into homewares. Clean, simple lines with an emphasis on natural textiles including marble and metal.

FUTURE AND FOUND
225A Brecknock Road
London N19 5AA
futureandfound.com
+44 (0)20 7276 4772
A collection of greys and neons, all beautifully photographed.

H&M HOME
www.hm.com
Global fashion giant H&M have a well-edited home department offering great-value 100% linen bedding in black, dark grey and light grey shades. Also cushions, throws and rugs in a monochrome palette.

HEM
www.hem.com
Based in Berlin with an international team of designers, Hem offers timeless and original designs. Not everything here is grey but if you want it in grey they will have it, and well-made too.

HOME STORIES
www.homestories.com
Brooklyn-based store offering serene, minimalist tableware and furnishings in umpteen shades of grey.

IN HOUSE JUNKIE
www.inhousejunkie.co.uk
There is something for every self-styled house junkie here. Most items have a lightly industrial feel and there are lots of grey and metal items.

LITTLE GREENE
www.littlegreene.com
Their Grey capsule paint collection consists of 28 shades – light, dark, cool and warm-toned – of which French Grey is the most poular.

MADE.COM
www.made.com
A huge range of affordable furniture in varying shades of grey, this online store is going from strength to strength. Check the website for details of their UK showrooms.

MENU
www.store.menudesignshop.com
Lots of concrete and grey furniture as well as the more classic Danish architectural monochrome pieces including pendant lighting and soft furnishings.

NORDIC HOUSE
www.nordichouse.co.uk
+44 (0)1872 223220
Owners Sandie and Alan live in Cornwall but spent years working in Sweden and their collection encompasses both aesthetics. Expect to find lots of textiles in pale and dark greys, candles, cushions and even carved wall panels.

NORMANN COPENHAGEN
www.normann-copenhagen.com
If you want a grey washing up bowl or a grey tray, this Danish brand is the place to come. Grey sofas a given.

PAPERS AND PAINTS
4 Park Walk
London SW10 0AD
www.papersandpaints.co.uk
Paint and colour consultancy for historic buildings. Their 12 'pure greys' are simple mixes of black and white and read as true neutrals.

RESTORATION HARDWARE
www.restorationhardware.com
Coast-to-coast US home furnishings brand offering classic, well-designed furnishings, lighting, tableware and everything else for the home.

ROCKETT ST GEORGE
www.rockettstgeorge.co.uk
Uber-cool homewares store where everything is set on a black background. There is a definite slant to the grey end of the colour chart, but this is also a good place to find neon and other colours to go with it.

ROSE AND GREY
www.roseandgrey.co.uk
A mix of vintage and contemporary with a Scandinavian flavour. Put grey into the search engine and you will come up with a pleasing mix of wallpaper, mirrors, rugs and furniture.

ROWEN AND WREN
www.rowenandwren.co.uk
+44 (0)1276 451 077
Lots of things you won't find anywhere else here. Colours are muted, designs are eclectic and there's an emphasis on quality. Much of the collection is photographed against a grey background, so if that's what you have you know these products will go perfectly.

SKANDIVIS
www.skandivis.co.uk
+44 (0)845 226 3104
Danish owner Toni Kay has put together a collection with a predominantly Scandinavian feel so expect to find lots of grey with the odd pop of muted colour.

SKANDIUM
86 Marylebone High Street
London W1U 4QS
skandium.com
+44 (0)20 7590 0030
Opened in 1999 by three Scandis aiming to be the best retailer of Scandinavian design and furniture in the UK. The staff are knowledgeable, the store is gorgeous and most of it is pleasingly monochrome.

STORY NORTH
www.storynorth.com
+44 (0)7825 545 469
Owner Samantha Osk Denidottir has an Icelandic mother and an English father. Her store concentrates on Nordic designs and, as such, has lots of monochrome and grey.

WAFFLE DESIGN
www.waffledesign.co.uk
+44 (0)7929 983628
Organic cotton rugs, cushions and throws made from a soft waffle weave. Lots of grey with other colours woven in.

WESTELM
www.westelm.com and co.uk
This US homeware chain has stores across the US and has recently opened in the UK, selling furniture with a mid-century feel. Lots of grey in the soft furnishings.

WOVEN
263 Fulham Road
London SW3 6HY
www.woven.co.uk
+44 (0)20 7193 0505
A huge selection of rugs in all shapes and sizes and shades of grey with every accent colour you can imagine.